I ♥ MY WOK

I  MY WOK

MORE THAN 100 FRESH,
FAST AND HEALTHY RECIPES

NICOLA GRAIMES

NOURISH
EAT WELL, LIVE WELL

First published in the UK and USA in 2017 by
Nourish, an imprint of Watkins Media Limited
19 Cecil Court
London WC2N 4EZ

enquiries@nourishbooks.com

Managing Editor: Rebecca Woods
Design: Karen Smith
Studio photography: William Lingwood
Photograph on page 2: shutterstock.com
Food Stylist: Marie-Ange LaPierre
Prop Stylist: Helen Trent

A CIP record for this book is available from
the British Library

ISBN: 978-1-84899-329-7

10 9 8 7 6 5 4 3 2 1

Typeset in Futura

Colour reproduction by Scanhouse, Malaysia
Printed in China

PUBLISHER'S NOTE
While every care has been taken in compiling the
recipes for this book, Watkins Media Limited, or any
other persons who have been involved in working
on this publication, cannot accept responsibility for
any errors or omissions, inadvertent or not, that may
be found in the recipes or text, nor for any problems
that may arise as a result of preparing one of these
recipes. If you are pregnant or breastfeeding or
have any special dietary requirements or medical
conditions, it is advisable to consult a medical
professional before following any of the recipes
contained in this book.

NOTES:
Unless otherwise stated:
• Use medium fruit and vegetables
• Use fresh ingredients, including herbs and spices
• Do not mix imperial and metric measurements
• All recipes serve 4 people

1 teaspoon = 5ml
1 tablespoon = 15ml
1 cup = 240ml

nourishbooks.com

SYMBOL KEY

Dairy-free

Nut-free (coconut is being treated as a nut in
this book, so recipes with coconut milk and
coconut/groundnut oil have not been labelled
as nut-free)

Wheat-free

Vegetarian (no meat, game or seafood, but
can contain dairy and egg products)

Vegan (no meat, game, seafood, honey,
dairy or egg products)

CONTENTS

INTRODUCTION

The wok has been an essential piece of equipment in Asian homes for centuries. Yet, despite this ancient lineage, the wok fits perfectly into today's Western-style kitchens and with contemporary styles of cooking.

The great beauty of the wok lies in its simple basic design, which has remained largely unchanged since its conception. While in the Western kitchen its role is often restricted to stir-frying, it is far more versatile. It also makes the ideal tool for steaming, blanching, braising, deep-frying and even for smoking food.

A wok, particularly when it is used for stir-frying, is the key to meals that are not only quick and easy to prepare, but also have the bonus of being healthy. This is largely because the shape of a wok lends itself so well to stir-frying, in which the food cooks rapidly in the minimum amount of oil, helping to keep fat levels down and to retain essential nutrients.

The recipes in this book reflect the true versatility of the wok. They present a huge variety of mouthwatering ways of preparing meat, poultry, fish, vegetables and rice and noodles, as well as soups, dim sum and other appetizers. Inspired by the traditions of some of the world's great cuisines, most notably those of Far Eastern countries such as China, Japan, Thailand, India, Vietnam and Indonesia, they offer even the most inexperienced cook the route to serving up a feast.

CHOOSING A WOK

Although all woks are basically of the same design, there are a few considerations to make when buying one, such as size, manufacturing material and shape:

If you only intend to buy one wok, choose one that lends itself to a wide range of cooking methods and that's not too small – preferably about 30–35cm/12–14in in diameter. Remember that it is better to have a large wok with a small amount of food in it than vice versa, especially when stir-frying.

A wok will usually have one of two types of handle: a single, long handle or two short, rounded handles on either side. The style you opt for is largely a matter of personal preference, although a single, long handle is generally better for stir-frying, as it distances you from the dangers of any spitting fat, makes it easier for you to toss around the ingredients being cooked and allows you to pick up the wok with one hand. Two-handled models, however, do tend to be more stable, which can be an important attribute when deep-frying or steaming.

Originally, woks were made from cast iron, which retains heat well but makes for a very heavy pan that is difficult to lift. The best modern woks are made from lightweight carbon steel, which is a good heat conductor and is non-stick when seasoned properly (see page 8). Stainless steel and aluminium woks are lighter still, but tend to scorch and blacken. Non-stick woks may seem like a good idea and are becoming increasingly popular, but bear in mind that they need special care to prevent scratching. Electric woks are convenient, but make sure that you choose the highest wattage possible, since some models do not heat up sufficiently for successful wok cooking.

Shape is another important consideration. Woks come with either a rounded bottom or a flat bottom. A round-bottomed wok is ideal for use on a gas hob, as its shape allows the heat to spread evenly over the surface for rapid cooking, but you will need a wok stand (see page 9) to hold the wok stable while cooking. Flat-bottomed woks are best for electric hobs or induction cookers, since they allow better direct contact with the heat source and they are independently stable. Whatever shape you opt for, make sure your wok has deep sides, making stir-frying and deep-frying easier and to prevent spillage.

SEASONING A WOK

Your new wok, with the exception of non-stick ones, will need cleaning and seasoning before use. Manufacturers often coat a wok in a protective layer of mineral oil that will need to be removed. To do this:

- Scrub the wok well with hot, soapy water, a kitchen cleanser or bicarbonate of soda/baking soda, then dry thoroughly over a low heat.

- Now season the wok by pouring in 2 tablespoons of cooking oil and rubbing it all over the inner surface using crumpled paper towels.

- Next place the wok over a low heat for 10–15 minutes, then wipe the inside again with more paper, held with tongs to avoid burning your fingers.

- Repeat the oiling, heating and wiping process until the paper towel comes away clean.

By seasoning your wok in this way regularly, a thin, oily coating will build up on the surface, making it non-stick and preventing rusting. Your wok will also become darker and, with continued use, will begin to impart a highly desirable 'smoky' flavour to food.

LOOKING AFTER YOUR WOK

Once your wok has been seasoned, it should ideally never be cleaned using a detergent; hot water and a cloth or bamboo brush should be all that are necessary to remove any stuck-on food.

After using, leave the wok to cool, then wash it in hot water and dry by placing over a low heat for a minute or two. You can then wipe the inside of the wok with a little cooking oil.

If your wok does rust, or if you find it very difficult to remove burnt-on food, you may need to use some detergent, but you will then have to re-season the wok before you can cook in it again.

COOK'S TOOLS

Specialist tools are not essential when cooking with a wok, but certain implements do make the process that much easier.

WOK STAND:

This metal ring is useful if you have a round-bottomed wok, since it makes it more stable on the stove, especially when deep-frying or steaming.

WOK LID:

Not all woks come with a lid, but one is useful and can be bought separately. A light, domed lid is essential for steaming (if you are not using a bamboo steamer) and also prevents sauces, soups and curries from drying out.

RACK:

This metal or wooden trivet can be used when steaming food to raise it above the water line. A rack is also useful when using a wok to smoke foods or for placing cooked food on to keep warm while something else is being cooked.

WOK STIRRER, SCOOP OR PADDLE:

This is indispensable for turning and tossing food when stir-frying. A spade-like implement, it has a slightly curved tip that matches the curve of the inside of the wok, making turning food much easier.

BAMBOO STEAMER:

These are available in a wide range of different sizes. The food is placed in the steamer, which is then placed on top of a wok of simmering water. A number of bamboo steamers can be stacked up on top of each other in order to steam a variety of different foods at the same time. Bamboo steamers come supplied with a lid to prevent the steam escaping.

CHOPSTICKS:

Long, wooden chopsticks are very useful for turning deep-fried foods.

SKIMMER OR LADLE:

A mesh ladle or metal slotted spoon is useful for lifting and draining food that has been stir-fried or deep-fried. Non-perforated ladles are good for adding liquid to a wok.

BAMBOO BRUSH:

This stiff, short brush is useful for cleaning a wok without scratching it or scrubbing off the seasoned surface.

CLEAVER:

This large, flat-bladed, all-purpose knife is perfect for cutting up lots of ingredients quickly and can then be used to scoop up the food and carry it to the wok. The side of a cleaver can also be used to crush garlic or to flatten meat and poultry.

COOKING TECHNIQUES
The wok is an extremely versatile piece of kitchen equipment that lends itself to a multitude of different cooking techniques.

STIR-FRYING
The secret to successful stir-frying lies in the preparation. Before you begin cooking, any solid food should be cut into uniform, bite-size pieces and all liquids and flavourings should be measured out and, in many cases, mixed together, ready to add to the wok.

- Meat and poultry should be cut into long, thin strips across the grain or into bite-size cubes, as these will cook quickly without drying out. Slicing is usually easier if the meat or poultry is placed in a freezer for about 30 minutes beforehand. Trim off any fat, as the fast cooking time means it will not cook through properly. Often meat and poultry are marinated before cooking to add extra flavour, but remember to drain off the marinade before stir-frying them.

- Certain oils are better than others for stir-frying. You should choose an oil that has a mild flavour and a high smoking-point, such as cold-pressed rapeseed oil, sunflower, vegetable, groundnut (peanut) or safflower. Coconut oil is also very stable at high temperatures

- When stir-frying, first heat your wok over a high heat until it starts to 'smoke', then, when it is really hot, add the oil and swirl it around to coat the inside of the wok. Flavourings, such as garlic and ginger, can then be added, but will only need stir-frying for a few seconds to prevent them burning. Add the ingredients that will take longest to cook next and toss them around constantly using a stirrer, scoop or paddle. Keep moving the food from the middle of the wok to the sides until it is cooked. You may sometimes need to add a little water or reduce the heat slightly if the stir-fry becomes dry or is scorching, but stir-fried food should never be allowed to become greasy or watery as this means the ingredients are being stewed rather than seared.

- Meat and poultry are generally cooked first – in batches if necessary, to prevent overcrowding in the wok. The meat should be allowed to sit in the wok briefly until lightly browned, and only then be stirred. This prevents it from sticking. After cooking, remove the meat from the wok and set on one side while you cook the remaining ingredients, the meat can then be returned to the wok, usually just prior to any liquid ingredients, such as soy sauce or a drained marinade.

- Only thick, firm fillets of fish are suitable for stir-frying and should be cut into large, even-sized pieces or, where appropriate, can be left whole. Like meat, fish should be left to brown lightly before moving or turning and even then great care should be taken to avoid breaking up the fish.

- Vegetables will also need to be cut into uniform-sized pieces. Broccoli, for example, should be cut into small florets with the stalks cut into thin sticks or slices. The stalk and leafy parts of vegetables such as pak choi/bok choy should be separated, with the stalk being thinly sliced and the leaves left whole or torn. Long vegetables, like beans, asparagus and spring onions/ scallions, are often cut on the diagonal, which not only looks appealing but also allows quicker cooking. Remember that hard vegetables, such as broccoli and carrots, require a longer cooking time than leafy vegetables, such as pak choi/ bok choy and spinach, which cook very quickly and so will only need to be added towards the end of the cooking time. Note that once liquid has been added, covering the wok with a lid can prevent any sauce that is formed from drying up as well as speeding up the final stages of cooking.

STEAMING

Steaming is a healthy, gentle method of cooking that helps to retain a food's nutrients and is low in fat. It is particularly good for cooking delicate fish, as well as vegetables and dim sum.

There are two main methods of steaming using a wok. The first is to place a plate of the food on a wooden or metal rack, which is balanced inside the wok, over about 5cm/2in of simmering water. The second method is to place the food in a bamboo steamer (see page 9), lined with baking paper, then place this into a wok of simmering water, about one-third full, so that the steamer is perched on the sloping sides of the wok, above the simmering water. The bottom of the steamer should never touch the water.

Remember to keep an eye on the water level in the wok while steaming, as it may need replenishing from time to time. Bamboo steamers can be stacked on top of one another to allow several different dishes or types of food to cook at the same time, but you may need to swap the position of the steamers around midway through cooking to allow all the food to cook evenly.

DEEP-FRYING

Woks are suitable for deep-frying and their shape means you need less oil than in a pan or fryer. Done correctly, deep-fried food should be crisp and golden, never greasy or soggy.

- The type of oil used is crucial – groundnut (peanut) and vegetable oils are ideal, due to their mild flavour and high smoking-point.

- The oil temperature is crucial to achieving a cooked centre and a crisp, not burnt, exterior. If you don't have a thermometer, try the bread test. Heat the oil until it gives off a haze and almost begins to smoke, then drop in a day-old cube of bread; if it bubbles all over and browns in 25–35 seconds, then the oil is hot enough.

- Make sure the wok is stable on the hob. To prevent oil splattering, ensure food is dry before placing it in the hot oil: if it has been marinated, drain before frying; if dipped in batter, allow any excess to drip off first.

- Deep-fry the food in batches to avoid it sticking together and the temperature of the oil dropping. Remove, using a mesh strainer, slotted spoon or spatula, and drain on paper towels. You may have to keep one batch of food hot while cooking the remainder as well as reheat the oil between batches.

BRAISING

'Red' braising is a technique used in Chinese cooking and involves stewing particularly tough cuts of meat and certain vegetables in a mixture of soy sauce, sugar and water, plus any flavourings, such as ginger and dried spices. The food then takes on a reddish-brown tinge during cooking, as well as the flavour of the spices and aromatics. The braising sauce can be saved and used again for another recipe, which increases the intensity of its flavour. Meat and poultry are often browned before braising, then cooked slowly in stock or another liquid until tender.

SMOKING

Smoking foods, such as meat, poultry or fish, is simple in a wok and gives a wonderful flavour.

- Line the wok and lid with foil to protect them, then put a smoking mixture, such as rice, tea, sugar and spices, into the base of the wok.
- Next marinate the food to be smoked first. Then put it on an oiled rack over the smoking mixture and cover it with a lid.
- Heat the wok until the mixture reaches smoking-point, then leave over a low heat until the food has cooked through and has a smoky flavour – make sure you open a window to keep the kitchen well ventilated.

APPETIZERS & SOUPS

Fragrant and nourishing, soups play a major role in Asian cuisine. Each country has its own, almost signature, soup ranging from the light, lemongrass-infused, chillied broths of Thailand to Malaysia's creamy, coconut-rich laksas and Japan's hearty, noodle-based ramens. You are likely to find that some of the soups in this chapter, such as Miso & Tofu Broth, are better served as a light snack or starter, while others, such as Coconut & Sweet Potato Noodle Soup or Malaysian Laksa, make a satisfying one-dish meal.

Similarly, the selection of appetizers will sit happily on menus for a whole host of different occasions. Many make good, quick-to-serve snacks, while others are perfect, palate-tingling openers to a dinner party. For classic dim sum, look no further than the recipes for Prawn & Ginger Dumplings and Yum Cha Salmon Buns. From Chinese Rice-paper Rolls with Caramelized Pork, to Asian Pea Broth with Pork Wonton or the ever-popular Thai Crab Cakes with Sweet Chilli Dip, this chapter will introduce you to the sheer excitement and variety of Asian food – and all you need is a wok.

GOLDEN PURSES

PREPARATION TIME 15 minutes

COOKING TIME 25 minutes   SERVES 4

1 tbsp sunflower oil, plus extra for deep-frying

2 cloves garlic, finely chopped

5 spring onions/scallions, finely chopped

5cm/2in piece fresh ginger, peeled and finely chopped

250g/9oz minced/ground chicken

2 tsp light soy sauce

2 tsp Chinese rice wine or dry sherry

20 wonton wrappers

salt and freshly ground black pepper

sweet chilli sauce (see page 20), for dipping

Heat a wok until hot. Add 1 tablespoon of oil, then the garlic, spring onions/scallions, ginger and chicken and stir-fry for 4 minutes until cooked through.

Pour in the soy sauce and wine and cook, stirring, for a further minute or until all the liquid has evaporated. Season to taste with salt and pepper.

Place one wonton wrapper on a flat surface, keeping the others covered with a damp cloth. Put a tablespoon of the chicken filling in the middle of the wrapper. Brush the wrapper with a little water, then gather the sides up around the filling and pinch together to make a bag, enclosing the filling. Set on one side, covered with a damp cloth. Repeat with the remaining wrappers and filling.

Heat enough oil in the wok to deep-fry the filled wonton. When the oil is hot enough to brown a day-old cube of bread in 35 seconds, add 3–4 wonton and cook for 1–2 minutes until golden. Drain on paper towels and keep warm. Repeat with the remaining wonton. Serve immediately with sweet chilli sauce, for dipping.

RICE-PAPER ROLLS WITH CARAMELIZED PORK

PREPARATION TIME 20 minutes, plus 1 hour marinating

COOKING TIME 10 minutes   SERVES 4

2 tbsp light soy sauce

2 tsp palm sugar or soft light brown sugar

2 tsp Thai fish sauce

500g/1lb 2oz lean pork fillets, cut into thin strips

2 tbsp sunflower oil

20 medium rice-paper wrappers

about 50ml/2fl oz hoisin sauce, plus extra
    for serving

70g/2½oz dried rice vermicelli noodles, cooked

fine strips of spring onion/scallion, mild red chilli
    and cucumber

handful of fresh coriander/cilantro leaves, to
    garnish (optional)

Mix together the soy sauce, sugar and fish sauce in a large shallow dish. Stir in the pork, so that it is well coated, and leave to marinate for 1 hour, spooning the marinade over the meat from time to time. Drain, reserving the marinade.

Heat a wok until hot. Pour in half the oil and swirl it around the wok, then stir-fry half of the pork for 3–4 minutes. Remove the meat from the wok with a slotted spoon and drain on paper towels. Heat the remaining oil in the wok, add the rest of the meat and stir-fry for 3–4 minutes.

Return the first batch of meat to the wok with the reserved marinade and cook over a high heat until caramelized.

Fill a heatproof bowl with just-boiled water. Put 2 rice-paper wrappers on top of one another and soak in the water for 20 seconds or until they are pliable and opaque. Carefully remove, using a spatula, drain for a second, and place flat on a plate.

Spread a teaspoonful of hoisin sauce over the double-layered wrapper, then top with a small bundle of noodles, a few strips of the caramelized pork and a few strips each of spring onion/scallion, red chilli and cucumber. Roll the wrapper around the filling, folding in the edges to enclose it. Repeat using the remaining wrappers and filling ingredients.

Slice the prepared rolls in half diagonally and serve, sprinkled with coriander/cilantro leaves, if you like, and with a bowl of extra hoisin sauce for dipping.

THAI CRAB CAKES

PREPARATION TIME 20 minutes, plus 30 minutes chilling
COOKING TIME 15 minutes   SERVES 4

250g/9oz fresh or canned white crab meat
250g/9oz pollock or other firm white fish fillet, skinned
2 cloves garlic, chopped
1 medium red chilli, deseeded and chopped
2 sticks lemongrass, peeled and finely chopped
5cm/2in piece fresh ginger, peeled and grated
large handful of fresh coriander/cilantro, finely chopped, plus extra whole leaves to garnish
1 free-range egg white
sunflower oil, for frying
salt and freshly ground black pepper

SWEET CHILLI DIP
3 tbsp mirin
3 tbsp rice vinegar
2 spring onions/scallions, finely sliced
1 tsp sugar
2 red chillies, deseeded and finely chopped

Put the crab meat, pollock, garlic, chilli, lemongrass, ginger, chopped coriander/cilantro and egg white in a food processor or blender. Season to taste with salt and pepper and process to form a coarse paste. Cover and chill for 30 minutes.

Meanwhile, make the sweet chilli dip. Mix together all the ingredients in a small bowl and set aside.

Heat 3 tablespoons of the oil in a large wok on a medium-high heat. Place 3–4 separate heaped tablespoons of the crab mixture into the wok and fry for 3–4 minutes on each side until golden. Drain on paper towels and keep warm. Repeat, cooking 3–4 cakes at a time and adding more oil to the wok if necessary. Garnish with the coriander/cilantro leaves and serve with the sweet chilli dip.

PRAWN & GINGER DUMPLINGS WITH CUCUMBER DIP

PREPARATION TIME 25 minutes

COOKING TIME 40 minutes   SERVES 4

200g/7oz raw king prawns/shrimp, peeled

2 spring onions/scallions, chopped

5cm/2in piece fresh ginger, peeled and finely chopped

2 tbsp light soy sauce

20 wonton wrappers

CUCUMBER DIP

½ small cucumber, deseeded and diced

5cm/2in piece fresh ginger, peeled and finely chopped

1 tsp palm sugar or soft light brown sugar

1 small red chilli, finely chopped

2 tbsp Thai fish sauce

juice of 1 lime

2 tbsp light soy sauce

Put the prawns/shrimp, spring onions/scallions, ginger and soy sauce in a food processor or blender and process to form a coarse paste.

Take one wonton wrapper, keeping the others covered with a damp cloth, and place a heaped teaspoon of the prawn/shrimp mixture in the middle. Brush the edges with a little water, then fold the wonton over the filling to form a triangle. Pick up the filled wonton, tap the bottom to flatten it, then pinch the edges together to seal. Cover with a damp cloth. Repeat with the remaining wonton wrappers and filling.

Place the filled wontons in a large bamboo steamer that is lined with baking parchment. (You may need to cook the wontons in batches.) Cover and steam over a wok of simmering water for about 8 minutes, adding extra water if needed to avoid boiling dry.

Meanwhile, mix together all the ingredients for the cucumber dip in a bowl. Serve the hot dumplings with the dip.

YUM CHA SALMON BUNS

PREPARATION TIME 25 minutes, plus 2 hours rising
COOKING TIME 30–45 minutes   SERVES 4

250ml/9fl oz/1 cup warm water
2 tbsp sugar
1 tsp dried yeast
350g/12oz/2½ cups plain/all-purpose flour
1 tsp salt
1 tbsp sunflower oil
1½ tsp baking powder
425g/15oz canned wild red salmon,
    bones and skin removed
5cm/2cm piece fresh ginger, peeled
    and finely chopped
6 spring onions/scallions, finely chopped
2 tbsp light soy sauce
salt and freshly ground black pepper

Prepare the dough by putting the warm water in a bowl and sprinkling over the sugar and yeast. Stir until the sugar dissolves, then cover the bowl and leave for 10 minutes until frothy. Sift the flour and salt into a large bowl and make a well in the middle. Pour the yeast mixture into the well and gradually mix in the flour to form a ball of soft dough. Turn out onto a lightly floured surface and knead for about 10 minutes until smooth and elastic, adding a little more flour if the dough is very sticky.

Wipe the inside of a large bowl with the oil, add the dough and turn it to coat with the oil. Cover the bowl with cling film/plastic wrap and leave in a warm place for about 2 hours, until the dough has doubled in size. Turn out onto a lightly floured surface. Then flatten the dough into a round, sprinkle with the baking powder, then fold over and knead for 5 minutes. Divide into 12 balls.

Mix together the salmon, ginger, spring onions/scallions and soy sauce and season to taste with salt and pepper.

Take a dough ball and flatten it into a round about 5mm/¼in thick. Put a large tablespoon of the salmon mixture in the middle, pull up the edges over the filling and press together to seal. Place the bun on a lightly floured surface and repeat with the remaining dough balls and filling.

Place the buns in a large bamboo steamer that has been lined with baking parchment. (You will need to cook the buns in batches.) Cover and steam over a wok of simmering water for about 15 minutes, adding more water if necessary to avoid boiling dry.

VEGETABLE SPRING ROLLS

PREPARATION TIME 20 minutes

COOKING TIME 20 minutes   SERVES 4

1 tbsp sunflower oil, plus extra for deep-frying

1 tsp sesame oil

2 carrots, cut into thin strips

150g/5½oz fine green beans,
    sliced and blanched

3 spring onions/scallions, finely sliced

5cm/2in piece fresh ginger, peeled
    and finely grated

2 cloves garlic, finely chopped

handful of beansprouts

1 tbsp dark soy sauce

50g/1¾oz dried vermicelli rice noodles, cooked
    and cut into 2.5cm/1in lengths

16 small spring roll wrappers

1 free-range egg white, lightly beaten

salt and freshly ground black pepper

SWEET PLUM DIP

6 tbsp sweet plum sauce

2 tbsp light soy sauce

Heat the oils in a wok until hot. Add the carrots, green beans and spring onions/scallions and stir-fry for 2 minutes. Add the ginger, garlic, beansprouts and soy sauce and stir-fry for another minute until the liquid evaporates. Transfer the vegetables to a bowl and set aside to cool. Stir the prepared noodles into the cooled vegetables. Season to taste with salt and pepper.

Lay a spring roll wrapper on a work surface, keeping the others covered with a damp cloth until ready to use. Place a heaped teaspoon of the vegetable and noodle mixture just in from the corner of the wrapper nearest to you, then fold the corner over the filling towards the middle. Fold in the two sides of the wrapper to enclose the filling, then continue to roll. Brush the far edge with a little egg white and fold over to seal. Repeat with the remaining wrappers and filling to make 16 rolls.

Heat enough sunflower oil to deep-fry the spring rolls in a wok. When the oil is hot enough to brown a cube of day-old bread in 35 seconds, fry 4–5 spring rolls in the oil until golden and crisp. Drain on paper towels and keep warm. Repeat with the remaining spring rolls, frying in batches of 4–5 at a time.

Mix together the ingredients for the dip in a small bowl and serve with the warm spring rolls.

MALAYSIAN LAKSA

PREPARATION TIME 20 minutes

COOKING TIME 16 minutes   SERVES 4

1 tbsp groundnut oil

450g/1lb skinless chicken breasts, cut into bite-size pieces

600ml/21fl oz/generous 2½ cups chicken stock

400g/14oz can coconut milk

3 kaffir lime leaves

2 pak choi/bok choy, halved lengthways

250g/9oz raw king prawns/shrimp, peeled

salt

175g/6oz rice noodles, cooked

handful of beansprouts

2 onions, chopped and fried until crisp

large handful of fresh coriander/cilantro, roughly chopped

1 long red chilli, deseeded and sliced

LAKSA PASTE

2 cloves garlic, sliced

2.5cm/1in fresh root ginger, peeled and chopped

2 candlenuts or 3 blanched almonds

2 red chillies, deseeded and chopped

3 shallots, chopped

1 tbsp tamarind paste

2 tbsp groundnut oil

2 tsp ground coriander

1 stick lemongrass, peeled and chopped

1 tsp ground turmeric

To make the laksa paste, put all the ingredients in a food processor or blender and process to form a coarse paste. Set on one side.

Heat a wok until hot. Add the oil, then the chicken and stir-fry for 3–4 minutes until it is cooked through. Remove from the wok using a slotted spoon and drain on paper towels.

Add the laksa paste to the wok and stir-fry for about 1 minute or until it smells aromatic. Pour in the stock and coconut milk and add the lime leaves. Bring to the boil, then reduce the heat and simmer for 7 minutes.

Add the pak choi/bok choy, prawns/shrimp and cooked chicken and cook for another 3 minutes. Season with salt to taste.

Divide the cooked noodles between four bowls and spoon the soup over the top. Sprinkle with the beansprouts, crispy onions, chopped coriander/cilantro and chilli and serve.

ASIAN PEA BROTH WITH PORK WONTON

PREPARATION TIME 25 minutes

COOKING TIME 12 minutes   SERVES 4

1 tbsp sunflower oil

1 tbsp butter

3 leeks, sliced

3 cloves garlic, finely chopped

5cm/2in piece fresh ginger, peeled and finely chopped

4 tbsp Chinese rice wine or dry sherry

1.5 litres/52fl oz/6½ cups vegetable stock

3 tbsp light soy sauce

300g/10½oz/1¼ cups frozen petit pois peas

salt and freshly ground black pepper

handful of Chinese chives, chopped, to serve

PORK WONTONS

250g/9oz lean pork fillet, roughly chopped

1 carrot, finely grated

2 cloves garlic, crushed

2 spring onions/scallions, finely chopped

1 tbsp plain/all-purpose flour

7cm/3in piece fresh ginger, peeled and finely chopped

1 tbsp light soy sauce

2 tsp Chinese rice wine or dry sherry

2 tsp sesame oil

24 wonton small wrappers

Put all the wonton ingredients, except the wrappers, in a food processor or blender and process to form a coarse paste. Take one wonton wrapper, keeping the others covered with a damp dish towel, and place a heaped tablespoon of the pork mixture in the middle. Brush the edges with a little water, then gather the sides up to enclose the filling and pinch together to seal. Cover with a damp cloth. Repeat with the remaining wonton wrappers and filling.

Place the wonton in a large bamboo steamer lined with baking parchment. (You may need to cook them in batches.) Cover and steam over a wok of simmering water for about 10 minutes, adding more water if necessary to avoid boiling dry.

Meanwhile, heat the oil and butter in a wok and stir-fry the leeks for 2 minutes. Add the garlic and ginger and stir-fry for a further 2 minutes. Add the wine and cook until most of it has evaporated. Add the stock and bring to the boil, then reduce the heat and simmer for 5 minutes. Add the soy sauce and petit pois peas and cook for another 2–3 minutes.

Season the soup to taste and pour into four warm serving bowls. Divide the pork wontons between the four bowls. Sprinkle over the chives and serve.

JAPANESE DASHI & NOODLE SOUP WITH TUNA

PREPARATION TIME 15 minutes, plus 1 hour marinating

COOKING TIME 10 minutes   SERVES 4

4 thick tuna steaks, about 140g/5oz each

4 tbsp dark soy sauce

1.5 litres/52fl oz/6½ cups hot water

10g/¼oz dashi stock powder

2 tbsp mirin

2 tbsp sunflower oil

4 spring onions/scallions, sliced diagonally

2 carrots, sliced

sesame seeds, for coating

175g/6oz fresh spinach, tough stalks removed and leaves shredded

175g/6oz dried somen noodles, cooked

1 large cooked beetroot/beet, thinly sliced

nori flakes, to garnish

MARINADE

1 tbsp mirin

3 tbsp dark soy sauce

½ tsp sansho pepper or freshly ground black pepper

Mix the marinade ingredients in a shallow dish. Add the tuna and spoon over the marinade to coat well. Leave to marinate for 1 hour, turning occasionally.

Mix together the soy sauce, hot water, dashi powder and mirin. Heat 1 tablespoon of oil in the wok, add the spring onions/scallions and carrots and stir-fry for 1 minute. Pour in the prepared dashi, mirin and soy stock and heat until it is just starting to boil. Reduce the heat and simmer for 5 minutes.

Meanwhile, remove the tuna from the marinade and dip both sides of each piece into a plate of sesame seeds until well coated. Heat a griddle pan until hot, brush the surface with oil and griddle the tuna for about 1 minute on each side. Slice and set on one side, keeping warm. Discard the marinade.

Stir the spinach and noodles into the hot liquid in the wok until the spinach wilts, then divide between four serving bowls. Place the tuna and beetroot on the top, sprinkle with the nori flakes and serve.

CHINESE SEAFOOD & SWEETCORN SOUP

PREPARATION TIME 15 minutes

COOKING TIME 13 minutes   SERVES 4

1 large free-range egg white

450g/1lb firm white fish, such as haddock or cod, cut into thick slices

2 tsp sunflower oil

3 shallots, chopped

2 tbsp Chinese rice wine or dry sherry

5cm/2in piece fresh ginger, peeled and grated

1.5 litres/52fl oz/6½ cups fish or chicken stock

1 tbsp light soy sauce or tamari

1½ tbsp cornflour/cornstarch

175g/6oz canned sweetcorn, drained and rinsed

4 small squid, gutted, cleaned and cut into rings

salt and freshly ground black pepper

2 spring onions/scallions, green part only, thinly sliced, to serve

Beat the egg white in a dish. Dip the fish into the egg white until coated and set on one side.

Heat the oil in a wok and stir-fry the shallots for 2 minutes. Pour in the wine and continue cooking until it has almost evaporated. Add the ginger, stock and soy sauce. Dissolve the cornflour/cornstarch in a little water and stir into the soup.

Bring to the boil, stirring, then reduce the heat and simmer for about 5 minutes until the soup thickens. Add the sweetcorn and fish and simmer for 3 minutes, then gently stir in the squid and cook for another 2 minutes.

Season to taste with salt and pepper and serve immediately with the sliced spring onions/scallions sprinkled over the top.

MISO & TOFU BROTH

PREPARATION TIME 10 minutes, plus
    5 minutes soaking
COOKING TIME 6 minutes   SERVES 4

3 tbsp dried wakame seaweed
1.2 litres/40fl oz/5 cups hot water
4–6 tbsp brown miso paste, according to taste
8 asparagus spears, trimmed and sliced
    diagonally
2.5cm/1in piece fresh ginger, peeled and sliced
    into thin strips
2 tbsp tamari
175g/6oz tofu, drained well and cubed
3 spring onions/scallions, white and green parts
    separated, sliced diagonally
½ tsp ground sansho pepper

Soak the wakame in hot water for 5 minutes until
softened. Drain and cut into small pieces.

Put the hot water and miso paste in a wok and
stir until the miso has dissolved. Add the wakame,
asparagus, ginger, tamari, tofu and white part
of the spring onions/scallions. Stir in the sansho
pepper and heat until the liquid is just beginning to
bubble. Reduce the heat and simmer for 3 minutes.

Pour the miso soup into four serving bowls.
Sprinkle with the green part of the spring onions/
scallions and serve immediately.

VEGETABLE RAMEN

PREPARATION TIME 20 minutes
COOKING TIME 5 minutes   SERVES 4

1 tbsp sunflower oil
1 tsp sesame oil
2 leeks, shredded
2 courgettes/zucchini, thinly sliced diagonally
8 button mushrooms, sliced
225g/8oz spinach, tough stalks removed and
    leaves shredded
handful of beansprouts
1.5 litres/52fl oz/6½ cups vegetable stock
3 tbsp light soy sauce
5cm/2in piece fresh ginger, peeled and grated
175g/6oz cooked ramen noodles
2 free-range eggs, hard-boiled and halved
2 spring onions/scallions, finely chopped
½ tsp dried chilli/hot pepper flakes

Heat the oils in a wok until hot. Add the leeks,
courgettes/zucchini and mushrooms and stir-fry for
2 minutes. Add the spinach and beansprouts and
stir-fry for a further minute. Add the stock, then add
the soy sauce and ginger. Bring up to the boil.

Divide the cooked noodles between four serving
bowls. Pour over the hot stock and vegetables.
Top each serving with half an egg, sprinkle with
the spring onions/scallions and chilli/hot pepper
flakes and serve.

COCONUT & SWEET POTATO NOODLE SOUP

PREPARATION TIME 20 minutes

COOKING TIME 25 minutes   SERVES 4

2 tbsp sunflower oil
2 large onions, chopped
2 cloves garlic, chopped
12 chestnut/cremini mushrooms, sliced
3 medium sweet potatoes, peeled and diced
1.2 litres/40fl oz/5 cups vegetable stock
250ml/9fl oz/1 cup coconut milk
2 tbsp light soy sauce or tamari
handful of fresh coriander/cilantro, chopped
175g/6oz dried rice noodles, cooked
salt and freshly ground black pepper

THAI RED CURRY PASTE
1 tsp dried shrimp paste
6 medium red chillies, deseeded and chopped
2 sticks lemongrass, peeled and chopped
3 shallots, peeled and chopped
juice of 2 kaffir limes and zest of 1
3 cloves garlic, chopped
1 tsp ground coriander
1 tsp ground cumin
2.5cm/1in piece fresh ginger, peeled and chopped
1 tbsp sunflower oil
1 tsp salt
1 tsp tamarind paste
½ tsp freshly ground black pepper

To make the red curry paste, wrap the shrimp paste in foil and place under a hot grill for 1 minute on each side. Leave until cool enough to handle, then unwrap the foil and place the cooked shrimp paste in a food processor or blender with the rest of the ingredients and process to form a coarse paste. Set on one side.

Heat 1 tablespoon of the oil in a wok and stir-fry half the chopped onions until crisp and golden. Remove from the wok and set on one side.

Heat the remaining oil in the wok. Add the rest of the chopped onion and stir-fry for 4 minutes. Add the garlic, mushrooms and sweet potatoes and stir-fry for another 2 minutes. Stir in half of the curry paste and cook for 3 minutes. The rest of the paste can be stored in the fridge for another recipe.

Pour in the vegetable stock and bring to the boil. Reduce the heat and simmer for 10 minutes. Stir in the coconut milk and soy sauce and cook for another 5 minutes. Season to taste with salt and pepper, then stir in the coriander/cilantro. Divide the noodles between four bowls and ladle the soup over the top. Sprinkle with the crispy onions and serve.

SALADS & SIDES

Salads do not usually spring to mind when considering what can be prepared in a wok, but this collection of tempting recipes, with their wide spectrum of colours, flavours and textures, should soon have you thinking very differently and will hopefully stimulate ideas for many new and delicious combinations.

The vibrant Stir-Fried Beetroot & Carrot Salad makes an excellent side dish, as does Warm Oriental Salad. For something a little more substantial, look no further than Soba Noodle & Chicken Salad, Vietnamese Hot Beef Salad, or the tastebud-tingling Thai-Style Squid Salad.

The collection of side dishes is equally varied and versatile. Included are Bombay Potatoes, Broccoli with Mustard Seeds, Chilli Bean Aubergine, Spinach with Shredded Coconut and the perennial favourite, Crispy Seaweed.

You could combine these recipes with a selection of other Asian dishes in this book to create a spectacular feast. Many may also be served up as an exciting and original side or accompaniment to a simple grilled piece of fish, roast meat or vegetarian alternative.

SOBA NOODLE & CHICKEN SALAD

PREPARATION TIME: 15 minutes

COOKING TIME: 8 minutes   SERVES 4

2 tbsp sunflower oil

4 skinless chicken breasts, about 125g/4½oz each, cut into strips

250g/9oz dried soba noodles

1 tbsp sesame oil

2 tbsp light soy sauce

2.5cm/1in piece fresh ginger, grated

1 tsp palm sugar or soft light brown sugar

5 spring onions/scallions, shredded

2 carrots, cut into thin sticks

5cm/2in piece cucumber, deseeded and cut into thin sticks

handful of fresh coriander/cilantro leaves

salt and freshly ground black pepper

Heat a wok until hot. Add half the sunflower oil, then half the chicken and stir-fry it for 4 minutes until lightly browned and cooked through. Remove from the wok using a slotted spoon, drain on paper towels and set on one side. Repeat with the remaining chicken.

Meanwhile, cook the soba noodles following the packet instructions, then drain and refresh under cold running water. Put into a serving bowl. Mix together the remaining sunflower oil, sesame oil, soy sauce, ginger and sugar and pour the mixture over the noodles. Add the spring onions/ scallions, carrots and cucumber and mix gently until combined.

Season the noodle salad to taste with salt and pepper, divide between four plates, top with the cooked chicken, sprinkle with the coriander/ cilantro leaves and serve.

VIETNAMESE HOT BEEF SALAD

PREPARATION TIME: 15 minutes, plus 1 hour marinating

COOKING TIME: 10 minutes   SERVES 4

450g/1lb rump steak, cut into thin strips

2 large handfuls of beansprouts

2 handfuls of mangetout/snow peas, trimmed and sliced diagonally

1 small cucumber, deseeded and sliced into ribbons with a potato peeler

1 tbsp sunflower oil

4 spring onions/scallions, sliced diagonally

1 long red chilli, deseeded and cut into strips

DRESSING

4 tbsp rice vinegar

4 tbsp Thai fish sauce

2 cloves garlic, crushed

2 tbsp sunflower oil

1 tsp sugar

juice from 2 limes

1 tbsp light soy sauce

Mix together the ingredients for the dressing in a small bowl. Pour half of the dressing into a shallow dish and add the beef. Spoon the dressing over the beef and marinate for at least 1 hour, then drain, discarding the marinade.

Arrange the beansprouts, mangetout/snow peas and cucumber on a serving platter.

Heat a wok until hot. Add the oil, then half the beef and stir-fry for 4–5 minutes. Remove the beef from the wok with a slotted spoon, drain on paper towels and set on one side. Repeat with the remaining beef. Leave to cool slightly.

Place the beef on top of the vegetables, spoon over the remaining dressing, sprinkle with the spring onions/scallions and chilli and serve.

THAI-STYLE SQUID SALAD

PREPARATION TIME: 20 minutes

COOKING TIME: 5 minutes   SERVES 4

12 small squid, gutted and cleaned,
tentacles separated

2 tbsp olive oil

2 large handfuls of baby spinach leaves, tough
stalks removed and leaves shredded

2 handfuls of rocket/arugula leaves

1 long red chilli, deseeded and cut into fine strips

large handful of fresh coriander/cilantro,
roughly chopped

handful of fresh basil leaves, torn

salt

DRESSING

3 tbsp lime juice

2 tbsp olive oil

2 tsp sesame oil

1 tbsp light soy sauce

2.5cm/1in piece fresh ginger, peeled and grated

1 small clove garlic, finely chopped

1 green chilli, deseeded and finely chopped

½ tsp palm sugar or soft light brown sugar

Mix together the ingredients for the dressing in a small bowl and set on one side.

Snip along the side edge of each squid pouch using scissors and open out to make a flat piece. Rinse and pat dry with paper towels. Cut into 3.5cm/1½in squares, then lightly score each piece in a criss-cross pattern. Season the squid squares and the tentacles with salt and drizzle over the olive oil then turn to coat the squid. Set on one side.

Heat the wok. Add half the squid and sear for 1½ minutes on each side. Remove from the wok using a slotted spoon, drain on paper towels and set on one side. Repeat with the remaining squid.

Arrange the spinach and rocket/arugula leaves on a serving platter, then pile the squid on top. Spoon over the dressing, garnish with the red chilli, chopped coriander/cilantro and basil leaves and serve.

WARM ORIENTAL SALAD

PREPARATION TIME: 10 minutes

COOKING TIME: 7 minutes   SERVES 4

2 large handfuls of fine green beans, trimmed

12 asparagus spears, trimmed and sliced
   diagonally

large handful of mangetout/snow peas, trimmed

2 tbsp olive oil

1 tbsp toasted sesame oil

5cm/2in piece fresh ginger, peeled and grated

2 tbsp soy sauce or tamari

1 large clove garlic, thinly sliced

Place the green beans and asparagus in a
bamboo steamer lined with baking paper. Cover
and steam over a wok of simmering water for
about 3 minutes. Add the mangetout/snow peas
and steam for another 1–2 minutes, until all the
vegetables are tender. Remove from the steamer,
arrange on a serving platter and keep warm.

Pour the water out of the wok and dry with
paper towels. Add the oils and heat gently. Add
the ginger, soy sauce and garlic and cook for
1 minute, until heated through. Pour the dressing
over the steamed vegetables, leave for a few
minutes to allow the flavours to mingle, then serve.

STIR-FRIED BEETROOT & CARROT SALAD

PREPARATION TIME: 15 minutes,
   plus cooling

COOKING TIME: 6 minutes   SERVES 4

3 tbsp coconut oil

3 Asian red shallots, sliced

400g/14oz raw beetroot/beets, peeled and
   cut into thin sticks

2 carrots, cut into thin sticks

juice and finely grated zest of 1 lime

large pinch of sugar

2 tsp sesame oil

handful of alfalfa sprouts

2 spring onions/scallions, thinly sliced

1 tbsp sesame seeds, toasted

salt and freshly ground black pepper

Heat the oil in a wok. Add the shallots and stir-fry
for 1 minute. Add the beetroot/beets and carrots
and stir-fry for another 3–4 minutes until tender.

Add the lime juice and zest, sugar and sesame
oil and stir until the vegetables are well coated.
Transfer the vegetables to a serving bowl and
leave to cool.

Just before serving, stir in the alfalfa and spring
onions/scallions. Sprinkle with sesame seeds,
season to taste with salt and pepper and serve.

VIETNAMESE BABY VEGETABLE SALAD

PREPARATION TIME: 15 minutes

COOKING TIME: 6 minutes SERVES 4

200g/7oz dried vermicelli noodles

1 tbsp groundnut oil

1 long red chilli, deseeded and chopped

2 lemongrass sticks, peeled and finely chopped

3 Asian red shallots, thinly sliced

6 baby courgettes/zucchini, sliced diagonally

6 baby corn, halved lengthways

1 small white cabbage, shredded

DRESSING

1 tbsp sesame oil

1 tbsp sunflower oil

1 tbsp light soy sauce

juice of 1 lime

½ tsp sugar

Cook the noodles following the packet instructions, drain and rinse under cold running water. Cut into shorter lengths and set aside. Mix together the dressing ingredients, season to taste, and set aside. Heat a wok until hot. Add the oil, then the chilli and lemongrass and stir-fry for a few seconds. Add the vegetables and stir-fry for 2 minutes. Leave to cool slightly, then stir in the cooked noodles and pile onto a serving platter. Pour over the dressing and serve.

Pictured on page 34

STIR-FRIED CHILLI MUSHROOMS

PREPARATION TIME: 10 minutes

COOKING TIME: 6 minutes   SERVES 4

2 tbsp sunflower oil

3 cloves garlic, chopped

200g/7oz shiitake mushrooms, halved or quartered if large

200g/7oz chestnut/cremini mushrooms, halved or quartered if large

1 long red chilli, deseeded and thinly sliced

3 tbsp light soy sauce or tamari

1 tbsp sweet chilli sauce

1 tbsp fresh lime juice

1 tbsp chopped fresh coriander/cilantro

salt and freshly ground black pepper

Heat the wok until hot. Pour in the oil and swirl it around to coat the wok. Add the garlic and stir-fry for 30 seconds then toss in both types of mushrooms and the chilli. Stir-fry over a high heat for 3 minutes.

Reduce the heat to medium-low then pour in the soy sauce, chilli sauce and lime juice. Season to taste and stir-fry for another minute. Serve sprinkled with coriander/cilantro.

CHILLI BEAN AUBERGINE

PREPARATION TIME: 10 minutes, plus 30 minutes salting

COOKING TIME: 20 minutes   SERVES 4

1 large aubergine/eggplant, quartered
lengthways and sliced

125ml/4fl oz/½ cup vegetable stock

4 tsp rice vinegar

3 tbsp Chinese cooking wine or dry sherry

1 tsp palm sugar or soft light brown sugar

2 tbsp light soy sauce

4 tbsp sunflower oil

2 cloves garlic, chopped

2.5cm/1in piece fresh ginger, roughly chopped

1 tbsp chilli bean paste

salt

Lay the aubergine/eggplant slices on a plate, sprinkle generously with salt, cover and set on one side for 30 minutes. Rinse well to remove the salt, pat dry using paper towels and set on one side.

Mix together the stock, rice vinegar, wine, sugar and soy sauce in a small bowl and set on one side.

Heat a wok until hot. Add the oil, then half the aubergine/eggplant and stir-fry for 5 minutes. Remove the aubergine/eggplant from the wok with a slotted spoon and set on one side. Put the remaining aubergine/eggplant in the wok, with more oil if necessary, and stir-fry for 5 minutes. Return the first batch of aubergine/eggplant to the wok.

Stir in the garlic and ginger, then pour in the stock mixture, add the chilli bean paste and cook for 2 minutes, stirring frequently, until the liquid has reduced and thickened and the aubergine/eggplant is tender.

PAK CHOI IN OYSTER SAUCE

PREPARATION TIME: 10 minutes

COOKING TIME: 4 minutes   SERVES 4

2 tbsp sunflower oil

2 cloves garlic, crushed

3 tbsp oyster sauce

1 tbsp hoisin sauce

1 tbsp light soy sauce

4 pak choi/bok choy, halved lengthways

Heat the wok until hot. Add the oil and garlic and stir-fry for a few seconds. Stir in the oyster sauce, hoisin sauce, soy sauce, pak choi/bok choy and 2 tablespoons of water. Stir-fry for 2–3 minutes until the pak choi/bok choy is tender, then serve.

SPINACH WITH SHREDDED COCONUT

PREPARATION TIME: 15 minutes

COOKING TIME: 6 minutes   SERVES 4

2 tbsp groundnut oil

1 large onion, chopped

1 tbsp yellow mustard seeds

10 curry leaves

1 long red chilli, deseeded and chopped

450g/1lb spinach, tough stalks removed and leaves shredded

grated flesh of ½ small fresh coconut

salt and freshly ground black pepper

Heat a wok until hot. Add the oil, then the onion and stir-fry for 3 minutes. Add the mustard seeds, curry leaves and chilli and stir-fry for another minute.

Toss in the spinach and stir-fry for 2 minutes until wilted, adding a little water if necessary. Stir in the coconut, season to taste with salt and pepper and serve.

BROCCOLI WITH MUSTARD SEEDS

PREPARATION TIME: 10 minutes

COOKING TIME: 6 minutes   SERVES 4

2 tbsp sunflower oil

1 tbsp yellow mustard seeds

5cm/2in piece fresh ginger, peeled and finely
    chopped

2 cloves garlic, finely sliced

350g/12oz broccoli, cut into small florets and
    stalks sliced

150ml/5fl oz/⅔ cup vegetable stock

salt and freshly ground black pepper

Heat the oil in a wok. Add the mustard seeds and
when they start to pop, add the ginger, garlic and
broccoli and stir-fry for 2 minutes.

Pour in the stock, bring to the boil, reduce the
heat, cover and simmer for 3–4 minutes or until
the broccoli is tender. Season to taste with salt and
pepper and serve.

CRISPY SEAWEED

PREPARATION TIME: 10 minutes

COOKING TIME: 5 minutes   SERVES 4

vegetable oil, for deep-frying

6 green cabbage leaves, finely shredded

salt

Pour the oil into a large wok until it is one-third
full. Heat until the oil is hot enough to brown a
day-old cube of bread in about 30 seconds. Toss
in the shredded cabbage and stir-fry for 2 minutes.
Scoop out using a slotted spoon, drain on paper
towels and set on one side.

Just before serving, heat the oil again, add the
cabbage and fry for about 1 minute until really
crisp. Remove from the wok, drain on paper
towels, season to taste with salt and serve.

COURGETTES IN YELLOW BEAN SAUCE

PREPARATION TIME: 5 minutes

COOKING TIME: 3 minutes   SERVES 4

3 tbsp yellow bean sauce

1 tsp chilli bean paste

2.5cm/1in piece fresh ginger, peeled and grated

1 tbsp sunflower oil

4 courgettes/zucchini, cut into thin sticks

Mix together the yellow bean sauce, chilli bean paste and ginger in a small bowl and set on one side.

Heat a wok until hot. Add the oil, then toss in the courgettes/zucchini and stir-fry them for 1 minute. Pour in the yellow bean mixture and stir-fry for another minute until the courgettes/zucchini are tender and thoroughly coated in the sauce, then serve.

GINGER-GLAZED SHALLOTS

PREPARATION TIME: 10 minutes

COOKING TIME: 8 minutes   SERVES 4

400g/14oz shallots, peeled

1 tbsp sunflower oil

1 tbsp softened butter

5cm/2in piece fresh ginger, peeled and finely chopped

1 tbsp clear honey

Plunge the shallots into a saucepan of just-boiled water for 4 minutes. Drain well, rinse under cold running water and set on one side.

Heat the oil in a wok. Add the shallots and stir-fry for 3 minutes, then stir in the butter. When the butter has melted, add the ginger, then the honey.

Continue to stir-fry the shallots for another minute until well coated in a glossy honey glaze, then serve.

BOMBAY POTATOES

PREPARATION TIME: 10 minutes, plus about
    30 minutes cooling
COOKING TIME: 20 minutes SERVES 4

6 medium-size potatoes, scrubbed and halved,
    if large
2 tbsp sunflower oil
1 large onion, sliced
1 tsp cumin seeds
1 tsp ground coriander
½ tsp hot chilli powder
1 tsp ground turmeric
5 fenugreek leaves
3 tomatoes, peeled, deseeded and chopped
salt

Cook the potatoes in plenty of boiling salted water
until tender. Drain and leave until cool enough to
handle. Peel the potatoes and cut into bite-size
cubes. Set on one side to cool completely.

Heat a wok until hot. Add the oil, then the onion
and stir-fry for 3 minutes. Toss in the cumin seeds,
ground coriander, chilli powder, turmeric and
fenugreek leaves and cook for another minute.

Stir in the tomatoes and 4 tablespoons of water,
season to taste with salt, and cook until the
tomatoes become very mushy. Stir in the potatoes,
heat through and serve.

HONEY-GLAZED CARROTS

PREPARATION TIME: 10 minutes
COOKING TIME: 5 minutes   SERVES 4

1 tbsp sunflower oil
3 carrots, cut into thin sticks
1 large clove garlic, chopped
handful of fresh rosemary, finely chopped
1 tbsp softened butter
1 tsp Dijon mustard
1 tbsp clear honey

Heat a wok until hot. Add the oil, then the carrots
and stir-fry them for 2 minutes. Add the garlic and
rosemary and cook for another minute.

Add the butter, mustard and honey, stir well to
coat the carrots in the mixture and cook over a
moderate heat until the carrots are tender.

MASALA CAULIFLOWER WITH ALMONDS

PREPARATION TIME: 15 minutes

COOKING TIME: 12 minutes   SERVES 4

1 cauliflower, cut into small florets

3 tbsp sunflower oil

1 tbsp black mustard seeds

1 tbsp coriander seeds, crushed

2 cloves garlic, chopped

½ tsp dried chilli/hot pepper flakes

1 tbsp lemon juice

salt and freshly ground black pepper

handful of flaked/sliced almonds, toasted, to serve

Put the cauliflower in a bamboo steamer lined with baking parchment. Cover and steam over a wok of simmering water for 2–3 minutes until slightly softened. Remove from the steamer and set on one side.

Pour out the water from the wok and wipe dry. Add the oil and heat, then add the mustard and coriander seeds, garlic and chilli/hot pepper flakes and stir-fry for a few seconds. Toss in the steamed cauliflower and stir well to coat it in the spices.

Add 3 tablespoons of water, cover the wok with a lid, and cook the cauliflower for about 8 minutes until tender, stirring occasionally. Stir in the lemon juice, season to taste with salt and pepper and serve, sprinkled with the almonds.

NOODLES & RICE

Noodles and rice are far more than just filling accompaniments to a meal. Fluffy grains of fragrant basmati rice, hearty udon and buckwheat noodles and silky threads of rice vermicelli shape the character of so much Asian cuisine. Without noodles and rice, many of the great dishes of Thailand, China, Japan, Vietnam, India, Indonesia and Malaysia would be inconceivable.

This chapter will show you just how versatile and satisfying noodles and rice can be by revealing the huge range of appetizing meals that can be created around these two most basic of staples. Among the varied recipes included are well-known classics such as Chinese Egg-fried Rice with Pork & Cashews, Pad Thai and, in the Indian style, Tandoori Chicken with Rice.

There are also recipes with that fuse European and Asian elements to create exciting new taste sensations. Chinese Mushroom Risotto combines Italian arborio rice with shiitake and oyster mushrooms and Chinese rice wine, while in the Oriental-style Paella a mixture of chicken, prawns/shrimp and rice is infused with aromatic Chinese five-spice.

CHICKEN CHOW MEIN

PREPARATION TIME: 15 minutes, plus 30 minutes marinating

COOKING TIME: 14 minutes   SERVES 4

3 tbsp mirin

3 tbsp light soy sauce

2 tsp cornflour/cornstarch

8 skinless, boneless chicken thighs, about 600g/1lb 5oz total weight, cut into bite-size pieces

300g/10½oz dried medium egg noodles

3 tbsp sunflower oil

2 cloves garlic, chopped

5cm/2in piece fresh ginger, peeled and finely chopped

1 carrot, diced

2 large handfuls of mangetout/snow peas, trimmed

3 Chinese leaves, sliced

5 spring onions/scallions, sliced

150ml/5fl oz/⅔ cup chicken stock

2 tbsp oyster sauce

1 tbsp light soy sauce

large handful of beansprouts

Mix together the mirin, soy sauce and cornflour/cornstarch in a shallow dish. Add the chicken and turn to coat in the marinade. Leave to marinate for 30 minutes, then drain, reserving the marinade.

Meanwhile, cook the noodles following the packet instructions. Drain, refresh under cold running water and set on one side.

Heat a wok until hot. Add the oil, then toss in the chicken and stir-fry it for 3–4 minutes until golden. Remove the chicken from the wok using a slotted spoon, drain on paper towels and set on one side. Put the garlic, ginger, carrot, mangetout/snow peas, Chinese leaves and spring onions/scallions into the wok and stir-fry for 2 minutes.

Return the chicken to the wok and pour in the stock, oyster sauce, soy sauce and reserved marinade. Stir-fry for about 2 minutes, until the liquid has reduced and thickened. Stir in the cooked noodles and beansprouts. Heat through and serve immediately.

MEE KROB

PREPARATION TIME: 10 minutes

COOKING TIME: 10 minutes   SERVES 4

6 tbsp Chinese rice wine or dry sherry

2 tbsp light soy sauce or tamari

1 tsp sugar

juice of 2 limes

groundnut oil, for deep-frying

1 bundle dried vermicelli rice noodles

2 skinless chicken breasts, about 150g/5½oz each, sliced into thin strips

2 cloves garlic, chopped

300g/10½oz raw king prawns/shrimp, peeled

5cm/2in piece fresh ginger, peeled and finely chopped

500g/1lb 2oz spinach, tough stalks removed and leaves shredded

½–1 tsp dried chilli/hot pepper flakes

salt

Mix together the wine, soy sauce, sugar and lime juice in a small bowl and set on one side.

Heat enough oil in a large wok to deep-fry the noodles. Add half the noodles and cook until they puff up and become light and crispy – this takes a matter of seconds. Remove from the wok using a slotted spoon, drain on paper towels and set on one side. Repeat with the remaining noodles.

Pour off all but 2 tablespoons of the oil out of the wok and reheat. Add the chicken and stir-fry for 3–4 minutes, then remove using a slotted spoon, drain on paper towels and set on one side.

Add the garlic, prawns/shrimp and ginger to the wok and stir-fry for 1 minute, then toss in the spinach with the wine mixture, followed by the chicken and the chilli/hot pepper flakes. Pour in 4 tablespoons of water and stir-fry for 2 minutes. Season to taste with salt.

Divide the stir-fry between four shallow serving bowls, top each with some of the crispy noodles and serve.

SINGAPORE NOODLES

PREPARATION TIME: 15 minutes, plus 30 minutes marinating

COOKING TIME: 15 minutes   SERVES 4

2 cloves garlic, crushed

5cm/2in piece fresh ginger, peeled and grated

3 tbsp light soy sauce

3 tbsp oyster sauce

250g/9oz pork fillet, thinly sliced across the grain

16 raw king prawns/shrimp, peeled

250g/9oz dried vermicelli rice noodles

2 tbsp sunflower oil

1 long red chilli, deseeded and thinly sliced

1 large carrot, cut into thin strips

handful of mangetout/snow peas, trimmed and halved diagonally

5 spring onions/scallions, sliced diagonally

1 tbsp curry power

½ tsp chilli powder

½ tsp turmeric

2 handfuls of beansprouts

Mix together the garlic, ginger, soy sauce and oyster sauce and divide between two bowls. Stir the pork into one bowl and the prawns/shrimp into the other, then leave to marinate for 30 minutes. Drain, reserving the marinade.

Cook the noodles following the packet instructions, then drain, refresh under cold running water and set on one side.

Heat a wok until hot. Add the oil, then toss in the pork and stir-fry it for 3 minutes. Remove from the wok using a slotted spoon and set on one side. Put the prawns/shrimp into the wok and stir-fry for 2 minutes, then remove using a slotted spoon and set on one side.

Reheat the wok, add the chilli, carrot, mangetout/snow peas and spring onions/scallions and stir-fry for 2 minutes. Stir in the curry powder, chilli powder, turmeric, 4 tablespoons of water and the reserved marinade, then return the pork and prawns/shrimp to the wok with the noodles. Add the beansprouts, stir-fry until heated through and serve.

UDON NOODLES WITH SPICED BEEF & BASIL

PREPARATION TIME: 15 minutes, plus 1 hour marinating

COOKING TIME: 10 minutes   SERVES 4

2 tbsp soy sauce

juice of 1 lime

500g/1lb 2oz sirloin steak, cut into strips across the grain

500g/1lb 2oz cooked udon noodles

200g/7oz fine green beans, trimmed

2 tbsp sunflower oil

2 small red chillies, deseeded and chopped

4 spring onions/scallions, sliced

1 tbsp Thai fish sauce

2 tsp palm sugar or soft light brown sugar

handful of fresh coriander/cilantro, chopped

handful of fresh basil leaves, torn

salt and freshly ground black pepper

Mix together the soy sauce and lime juice in a shallow dish. Season well with salt and pepper and add the steak. Stir until the steak is coated in the marinade. Leave to marinate for 1 hour. Drain, reserving the marinade.

Put the cooked noodles in a pan of boiling water and cook for 1 minute to separate them. Drain well, refresh under cold running water and set on one side. Plunge the green beans into a pan of boiling water for 2 minutes, then drain, refresh under cold running water and set on one side.

Heat a wok until hot. Add the oil, then toss in the beef and stir-fry for 2–3 minutes. Remove the beef from the wok using a slotted spoon and set on one side.

Put the chillies, spring onions/scallions and green beans into the wok and stir-fry for 1 minute. Add the fish sauce, reserved marinade and sugar. Stir, then return the beef to the wok with the noodles and heat through, stirring constantly. Season to taste with salt and pepper, then mix in the coriander/cilantro and serve with the basil scattered over.

YAKISOBA NOODLES

PREPARATION TIME: 15 minutes, plus 1 hour marinating time

COOKING TIME: 25 minutes   SERVES 4

350g/12oz firm tofu, drained, patted dry and cubed

250g/9oz dried ramen noodles

2 tbsp rice vinegar

1 tbsp tomato ketchup

2 tbsp vegetarian 'oyster' sauce

1 tsp soft light brown sugar

1 tbsp sunflower oil, plus extra for greasing

1 tbsp sesame oil

5cm/2in piece fresh ginger, peeled and finely chopped

1 red pepper, sliced

1 carrot, sliced diagonally

2 courgettes/zucchini, sliced diagonally

250g/9oz Chinese leaves, shredded

6 spring onions/scallions, white and green parts separated, sliced diagonally

handful of toasted sesame seeds

MARINADE

3 tbsp Japanese soy sauce

3 cloves garlic, finely chopped

2 tbsp sweet chilli sauce

3 tbsp mirin

Mix together the marinade ingredients in a dish. Add the tofu and stir to coat. Leave for 1 hour, turning the tofu occasionally. Drain, reserving the marinade.

Preheat the oven to 180°C/350°F/Gas 4. Put the tofu on a lightly oiled baking sheet and roast in the oven for 20 minutes, turning halfway, until crisp and golden.

Meanwhile, cook the noodles following the packet instructions. Rinse, refresh under cold running water and set on one side. Mix together the rice vinegar, ketchup, oyster sauce and sugar in a small bowl and set on one side.

Heat a wok until hot. Add the oils, then toss in the ginger, red pepper and carrot and stir-fry for 1 minute. Add the courgettes/zucchini, Chinese leaves and the white part of the spring onions/scallions and stir-fry for another 2 minutes.

Mix the rice vinegar mixture and the reserved marinade together and add to the wok with the cooked noodles. Toss over a medium heat until combined and heated through, then serve with the tofu, sesame seeds and the green part of the spring onions/scallions sprinkled over the top.

PAD THAI

PREPARATION TIME: 15 minutes
COOKING TIME: 8 minutes   SERVES 4

250g/9oz dried medium rice noodles
1 tbsp sunflower oil
3 cloves garlic, finely chopped
1 large carrot, cut into thin strips
4 spring onions/scallions, white and green parts separated, sliced diagonally
1 long red chilli, finely sliced
juice of 1 lime
3 tbsp light soy sauce
2 tbsp rice vinegar
2 tbsp sweet chilli sauce
2 free-range eggs, lightly beaten
handful of beansprouts
handful of roasted peanuts, crushed
large handful of fresh coriander/cilantro, finely chopped
salt and freshly ground black pepper

Cook the noodles following the packet instructions. Drain, refresh under cold running water and set on one side.

Heat a wok until hot. Add the oil, then the garlic, carrot, white part of the spring onions/scallions and chilli and stir-fry for 1 minute. Stir in the lime juice, soy sauce, rice vinegar and chilli sauce.

Add the cooked noodles and stir gently to avoid breaking up the noodles until mixed with the other ingredients. Push the noodles to one side and add the eggs. Stir gently until the eggs are incorporated into the noodles and lightly set. Season to taste with salt and pepper.

Sprinkle over the beansprouts, peanuts, coriander/cilantro and the green part of the spring onions/scallions and serve.

Pictured on page 52

RAINBOW VEGETABLE NOODLES

PREPARATION TIME: 10 minutes

COOKING TIME: 12 minutes   SERVES 4

250g/9oz dried thick egg noodles

1 tbsp sunflower oil

2 tsp sesame oil

8 medium broccoli florets, cut into small florets and stalks thinly sliced

2 handfuls of fine green beans, trimmed and sliced

1 carrot, finely shredded

1 red pepper, deseeded and diced

2 cloves garlic, chopped

5cm/2in piece fresh ginger, peeled and grated

2 tbsp light soy sauce

4 tbsp fresh apple juice

2 tbsp sesame seeds, toasted

Cook the noodles following the packet instructions. Drain, refresh under cold running water and set on one side.

Heat a wok until hot. Add the oils, then toss in the broccoli and green beans and stir-fry for 2 minutes. Add the carrot and pepper and stir-fry for another 2 minutes, then add the garlic and ginger and stir-fry for a further minute.

Pour in the soy sauce and apple juice and add the cooked noodles, then stir-fry for another 2 minutes, adding a little water if the noodles appear too dry. Serve sprinkled with the toasted sesame seeds.

NOODLES WITH CORIANDER PESTO

PREPARATION TIME: 20 minutes

COOKING TIME: 10 minutes   SERVES 4

250g/9oz dried medium egg noodles

1 tbsp sunflower oil

1 red pepper, deseeded and sliced

12 baby corn, halved lengthways

handful of beansprouts

2 tbsp sesame seeds, toasted

handful of fresh coriander/cilantro leaves

CORIANDER PESTO

2 handfuls of fresh coriander/cilantro, roughly chopped

3 cloves garlic, chopped

1 long red chilli, chopped

5 tbsp sunflower oil

5cm/2in piece fresh ginger, peeled and grated

juice and finely grated rind of 2 limes

2 tbsp light soy sauce

1 tbsp sesame oil

Put all the ingredients for the pesto in a food processor or blender and process to form a thick paste.

Cook the noodles following the packet instructions. Drain, refresh under cold running water and set on one side.

Heat a wok until hot. Add the oil, then toss in the pepper and baby corn and stir-fry for 2 minutes. Add the cooked noodles and 4–6 tablespoons of the pesto. Toss the noodles until they are coated in the pesto and heated through, adding a splash of water if needed.

Remove from the heat and stir in the beansprouts. Serve immediately, with the sesame seeds and coriander/cilantro leaves scattered over the top.

EGG-FRIED RICE WITH PORK & CASHEWS

PREPARATION TIME: 15 minutes, plus 30 minutes cooling

COOKING TIME: 18 minutes   SERVES 4

325g/11½oz/1½ cups basmati rice, rinsed

2 tbsp groundnut oil

1 clove garlic, chopped

2.5cm/1in piece fresh ginger, peeled and finely chopped

4 spring onions/scallions, sliced diagonally

8 baby corn, sliced lengthways

300g/10½oz Chinese barbecued pork, diced

2 tbsp Chinese cooking wine or dry sherry

2 tbsp light soy sauce

2 tsp sesame oil

2 free-range eggs, lightly beaten

large handful of toasted unsalted cashew nuts, chopped

salt and freshly ground black pepper

Put the rice in a saucepan and cover with 750ml/26fl oz/3¼ cups water. Season to taste with salt and bring to the boil, then reduce the heat to low, cover and simmer for 10–12 minutes until the water has been absorbed and the rice is tender. Remove the pan from the heat and leave to stand, covered, for 5 minutes. Transfer the rice to a bowl and leave to cool, fluffing it up occasionally with a fork.

Heat the oil in a wok. Add the garlic, ginger and spring onions/scallions and stir-fry for 30 seconds. Add the baby corn and pork and stir-fry for 2 minutes.

Add the cooked, cooled rice and stir-fry for 2 minutes, then pour in the wine, soy sauce and sesame oil. Add the eggs, leave for a few seconds to allow them to start to cook, then stir-fry until mixed throughout the rice. The rice should be piping hot. Season to taste with salt and pepper and serve, topped with the toasted cashew nuts.

ORIENTAL-STYLE PAELLA

PREPARATION TIME: 20 minutes

COOKING TIME: 40 minutes   SERVES 4

2 tbsp coconut oil

115g/4oz shiitake mushrooms, thickly sliced

1 red pepper, deseeded and diced

2 handfuls of fine green beans, trimmed and halved

1 onion, finely chopped

2 cloves garlic, chopped

5cm/2in piece fresh ginger, peeled and finely chopped

1 tsp ground turmeric

½ tsp Chinese five-spice

300g/10½oz/1½ cups paella rice, rinsed

4 tbsp Chinese rice wine or dry sherry

1 litre/35fl oz/4⅓ cups hot chicken or vegetable stock

85g/3oz/⅔ cup frozen petit pois peas

100g/3½oz Chinese leaves, roughly chopped

200g/7oz cooked king prawns/shrimp, peeled

2 cooked skinless chicken breasts, about 150g/5½oz each, cut into bite-size pieces

2 tsp sesame oil

salt and freshly ground black pepper

Heat a wok until hot. Add the coconut oil, then toss in the mushrooms, red pepper and green beans and stir-fry for 3 minutes. Remove from the wok using a slotted spoon and set on one side.

Put the onion into the wok and stir-fry for 4 minutes. Add the garlic, ginger, turmeric and five-spice and stir-fry for 30 seconds. Tip in the rice and stir-fry for 2 minutes until the grains are translucent.

Stir in the wine and cook until most has evaporated, then add 250ml/9fl oz/1 cup of the stock. Bring to the boil, then reduce the heat and simmer for 3 minutes, stirring, until most of the stock has been absorbed by the rice. Continue to simmer and add the stock in batches, stirring frequently, for 15–20 minutes, until the rice is cooked but still has some bite.

Just before you stir in the last batch of stock, add the peas, Chinese leaves, prawns/shrimp, chicken and reserved vegetables and stir in the sesame oil. Cover and leave to cook for about 3 minutes until the rice is tender and the chicken is cooked through. Add a little more water if necessary to keep the rice moist but not sloppy. Season to taste and serve.

TANDOORI CHICKEN WITH RICE

PREPARATION TIME: 10 minutes

COOKING TIME: 25 minutes   SERVES 4

325g/11½oz/1½ cups basmati rice, rinsed

1 tbsp groundnut oil, plus extra for frying

2 tbsp butter

1 onion, finely chopped

1 tbsp tandoori curry powder

500g/1lb 2oz cooked tandoori chicken pieces

salt and freshly ground black pepper

Put the rice in a saucepan and cover with 750ml/26fl oz/3¼ cups water. Season to taste with salt and bring to the boil, then reduce the heat to low, cover and simmer for 10–12 minutes until the water has been absorbed and the rice is tender. Remove the pan from the heat and leave to stand, covered, for 5 minutes. Transfer the rice to a bowl and leave to cool, fluffing it up occasionally with a fork.

Heat the oil and butter in a large wok, add the onion and stir-fry for 5 minutes, then stir in the curry powder.

Mix in the cooked, cooled rice and heat through thoroughly, stirring constantly, until it is coated in the buttery spice mixture. The rice should be piping hot. Season to taste with salt and pepper, then transfer to a serving bowl and keep warm.

Pour a little extra oil into the wok and add the chicken. Stir-fry until heated through. Lift out of the wok with a slotted spoon, place on top of the rice and serve.

PRAWN & COCONUT PILAF

PREPARATION TIME: 10 minutes

COOKING TIME: 24 minutes   SERVES 4

325g/11½oz/1½ cups basmati rice, rinsed

1 cinnamon stick

2 whole cloves

2 tbsp coconut oil

1 onion, finely chopped

1 tbsp cumin seeds

3 cloves garlic, chopped

7cm/3in piece fresh ginger, peeled and grated

10 curry leaves

1 tsp ground turmeric

8 chestnut/cremini mushrooms, sliced

400g/14oz can coconut milk

300g/10½oz raw king prawns/shrimp, peeled

175g/6oz spinach, tough stalks removed and leaves shredded

salt and freshly ground black pepper

Put the rice, cinnamon stick and cloves in a saucepan and cover with 750ml/26fl oz/ 3¼ cups water. Season to taste with salt and bring to the boil, then reduce the heat to low, cover and simmer for 10–12 minutes until the water has been absorbed and the rice is tender. Remove the pan from the heat and leave to stand, covered, for 5 minutes.

Meanwhile, heat a wok until hot. Add the oil, then toss in the onion and stir-fry it for 3 minutes. Add the cumin seeds, garlic, ginger, curry leaves and turmeric and stir-fry for 30 seconds. Add the mushrooms and cook for another minute.

Pour in the coconut milk and 5 tablespoons of water. Bring to the boil, then reduce the heat and simmer for 5 minutes. Stir in the cooked rice, the prawns/shrimp and the spinach and cook, stirring frequently, for another few minutes until the rice is heated through thoroughly, the prawns/shrimp are pink and the spinach has wilted. Season to taste with salt and pepper and serve.

INDONESIAN RICE

PREPARATION TIME: 15 minutes

COOKING TIME: 18 minutes   SERVES 4

325g/11½oz/1½ cups long-grain rice, rinsed

750ml/26fl oz/3¼ cups vegetable stock

1 cinnamon stick

2 sticks lemongrass, peeled

2 whole cloves

2 tbsp sunflower oil

4 Asian red shallots, chopped

2 cloves garlic, chopped

5cm/2in piece fresh ginger, peeled and finely chopped

1 tbsp ground coriander

2 tsp ground cumin

250ml/9fl oz/1 cup coconut milk

handful of fresh coriander/cilantro, roughly chopped

1 long red chilli, deseeded and thinly sliced

1 onion, roughly chopped and fried until crisp and golden

1 carrot, cut into ribbons with a vegetable peeler

salt and freshly ground black pepper

Put the rice in a saucepan and cover with the stock. Add the cinnamon, 1 stick of lemongrass and the cloves. Bring to the boil, then reduce the heat to low, cover and simmer for 10–12 minutes until the water has been absorbed and the rice is tender. Remove the pan from the heat and leave to stand, covered, for 5 minutes. Transfer the rice to a bowl, remove and discard the cinnamon, lemongrass and cloves and leave the rice to cool, fluffing it up from time to time with a fork.

Finely chop the remaining lemongrass. Heat a wok until hot, add the oil, then toss in the shallots and stir-fry for 2 minutes. Add the garlic, ginger, ground coriander and cumin and the chopped lemongrass and stir-fry for 30 seconds.

Stir in the coconut milk and the cooked rice and heat through thoroughly. The rice should be piping hot. Transfer to a warm serving bowl, season to taste with salt and pepper and mix in the chopped coriander/cilantro. Sprinkle over the chilli and crispy onions, arrange the carrot ribbons on top and serve.

CHINESE MUSHROOM RISOTTO

PREPARATION TIME: 15 minutes, plus 20 minutes soaking

COOKING TIME: 35 minutes   SERVES 4

12 dried shiitake mushrooms

2 tbsp sunflower oil

1 large onion, finely chopped

2 cloves garlic, chopped

5cm/2in piece fresh ginger, finely chopped

100g/3½oz chestnut/cremini mushrooms, sliced

140g/5oz oyster mushrooms, sliced

450g/1lb/2⅓ cups risotto rice

185ml/6fl oz/¾ cup Chinese rice wine or dry sherry

1.2 litres/40fl oz/5 cups hot vegetable stock

2 handfuls of basil leaves, torn

2 handfuls of fresh coriander/cilantro, roughly chopped

2 handfuls of Chinese chives, snipped

salt and freshly ground black pepper

soy sauce, for drizzling

Put the dried shiitake mushrooms in a bowl, pour over enough hot water to just cover and leave to soak for 20 minutes until softened. Drain, reserving the soaking liquor. Remove the mushroom stalks and discard them. Slice the caps and set on one side.

Heat a wok until hot. Add the oil, then toss in the onion and stir-fry it for 4 minutes. Add the garlic, ginger and all the mushrooms and stir-fry for 3 minutes. Mix in the rice and cook for a further minute until the grains are translucent.

Pour in the wine and bring to the boil, then reduce the heat and cook, stirring, until the wine is absorbed. Strain the mushroom soaking liquor and combine with the stock. Add the stock a little at a time and simmer, stirring, for 20–25 minutes until all the liquid has been absorbed and the rice is tender. Season to taste with salt and pepper and stir in the basil, fresh coriander/cilantro and chives. Drizzle a little soy sauce over the top and serve.

MEAT

India, Korea, China, Japan, Malaysia and Indonesia are just a few of the Asian countries that have inspired the recipes in this chapter. Each national cuisine has its own distinctive characteristics, but they all demonstrate the subtle balance of taste sensations – sweet, sour, hot and salty – that are key to Asian cooking.

Asia's many tempting meat dishes clearly demonstrate the diversity of food from this corner of the world. Quickly prepared stir-fries and slow-cooked stews are created by infusing carefully selected cuts of beef, pork, lamb and other meats with flavourings such as tamarind, lime, lemongrass, chillies, soy sauce, mirin, garlic, ginger and coconut. Try the classic Indian curry, Lamb Rogan Josh, in which succulent chunks of meat are simmered in a spicy, yogurt sauce, or travel to China for fragrant Five-Spice Pork with Choi Sum, or to Japan for rejuvenating Beef with Lime & Sesame Marinade.

Always choose a cut of meat that suits the cooking technique being used (see pages 11–13). Successful stir-frying demands really lean, tender meat, preferably cut across the grain to prevent it drying out. Marinating meat before cooking also helps to tenderize it and will add flavour, too.

PORK JUNGLE CURRY

PREPARATION TIME: 20 minutes

COOKING TIME: 22 minutes   SERVES 4

2 tbsp vegetable oil

650g/1lb 7oz lean pork loin fillet, cut into 2cm/3¾in cubes

1 large onion, finely sliced

300g/10½oz broccoli florets

2 cloves garlic, chopped

350ml/12fl oz/1½ cups hot chicken stock

1 tbsp Thai fish sauce

20g/¾oz candlenuts or almonds, ground

100g/3½oz canned bamboo shoots, drained and rinsed

juice of 1 lime

salt and freshly ground black pepper

JUNGLE CURRY PASTE

1 tbsp shrimp paste

6 medium red chillies, deseeded and chopped

6 shallots or 4 Asian red shallots

4 cloves garlic, chopped

2 sticks lemongrass, peeled and chopped

1cm/½in piece coriander/cilantro root, peeled and chopped

5cm/2in piece galangal, peeled and chopped

½ tsp salt

½ tsp freshly ground black pepper

1 tsp kaffir lime zest

To make the jungle curry paste, wrap the shrimp paste in foil, then place under a hot grill for 1 minute on each side. Leave until cool enough to handle, then unwrap the cooked shrimp paste and put it in a food processor or blender with the rest of the ingredients. Process to form a coarse paste.

Heat a wok until hot. Add the oil, then add half of the pork and stir-fry it for 3–4 minutes until browned. Remove from the wok with a slotted spoon and set on one side. Repeat with the remaining pork.

Add the onion to the wok and stir-fry for 3 minutes, then toss in the broccoli and cook, stirring, for another 2 minutes. Next, stir in the garlic and half of the curry paste and cook, stirring, for 3 minutes. (The rest of the curry paste can be stored in the refrigerator for another recipe.)

Return the pork to the wok with the stock, fish sauce, nuts and bamboo shoots and bring to the boil, then reduce the heat and simmer, covered, for 5 minutes. Stir in the lime juice, season to taste with salt and pepper and serve.

FIVE-SPICE PORK WITH CHOI SUM

PREPARATION TIME: 15 minutes

COOKING TIME: 40 minutes   SERVES 4

600ml/21fl oz/generous 2½ cups hot chicken stock

3 tbsp light soy sauce

6 tbsp Chinese rice wine or dry sherry

5cm/2in piece fresh ginger, finely chopped

2 star anise

1 tsp Chinese five-spice

4 large strips of orange zest

1 tbsp palm sugar or soft light brown sugar

1½ tbsp sunflower oil

600g/1lb 5oz pork tenderloin

5 spring onions/scallions, sliced diagonally

1 large red pepper, deseeded and sliced

350g/12oz choi sum (Chinese flowering cabbage), stalks sliced and leaves left whole

Put the stock, soy sauce, wine, ginger, star anise, five-spice and orange zest in a large saucepan. Bring to the boil, then stir in the sugar. Reduce the heat and simmer for 5 minutes, then strain and set on one side.

Heat a large wok until hot. Add the oil, then add the whole pork piece and stir-fry over a high heat until browned on all sides. Pour in the stock mixture, cover and simmer for 20 minutes, turning the pork from time to time.

Remove the pork from the wok with a slotted spoon, set on one side and keep warm. Add the spring onions/scallions, red pepper and choi sum to the wok and simmer for 4 minutes until tender. Slice the pork and divide between four warm serving bowls. Spoon over the vegetables and stock and serve.

SWEET & SOUR PORK

PREPARATION TIME: 15 minutes
COOKING TIME: 15 minutes   SERVES 4

5 tbsp fresh orange juice
3 tbsp light soy sauce
2 tbsp rice vinegar
1 tbsp runny honey
2 tsp cornflour/cornstarch
2 tbsp vegetable oil
600g/1lb 5oz lean pork loin fillet, thinly sliced
1 large onion, thinly sliced
8 chestnut/cremini mushrooms, sliced
2 carrots, sliced diagonally
2 courgettes/zucchini, sliced diagonally
large handful of beansprouts

Mix the orange juice, soy sauce, rice vinegar, honey and cornflour/cornstarch in a bowl and set aside.

Heat a wok until hot. Add the oil, then add half the pork and stir-fry it for 3–4 minutes until browned. Remove from the wok using a slotted spoon and set aside. Repeat with the remaining pork. Put the onion into the wok and stir-fry for 2 minutes. Add the mushrooms, carrots and courgettes/zucchini and stir-fry for another 2–3 minutes. Return the pork to the wok and stir in the beansprouts. Pour in the orange juice mixture and let it bubble, stirring, until the sauce has thickened. Add a little water if the sauce becomes too dry, then serve.

PORK & WOM BOK

PREPARATION TIME: 15 minutes, plus
    30 minutes marinating
COOKING TIME: 8 minutes   SERVES 4

1 free-range egg white, lightly beaten
4 tbsp Chinese rice wine or dry sherry
2 tbsp light soy sauce
1 tbsp cornflour/cornstarch
600g/1lb 5oz lean pork loin fillet, thinly sliced
2 tbsp sunflower oil
4 spring onions/scallions, sliced diagonally
2 cloves garlic, chopped
5cm/2in piece fresh ginger, peeled and finely
    chopped
5 wom bok leaves (Chinese leaves), shredded
handful of unsalted peanuts, toasted

Mix together the egg white, half the wine, soy sauce, cornflour/cornstarch and 4 tablespoons of water in a bowl. Add the pork and stir until well coated. Leave to marinate for 30 minutes.

Heat a wok until hot. Add the oil, then toss in the spring onions/scallions, garlic, ginger and wom bok and stir-fry for 30 seconds. Lift the pork out of the marinade using a slotted spoon, add to the wok and stir-fry for 3–4 minutes until browned. Pour in the remaining wine and marinade and stir-fry until reduced and thickened. Serve sprinkled with the toasted peanuts.

KOREAN-STYLE MARINATED PORK

PREPARATION TIME: 12 minutes, plus 1 hour marinating

COOKING TIME: 15 minutes   SERVES 4

650g/1lb 7oz lean pork loin fillet, sliced into strips across the grain

2 tbsp groundnut oil

3 spring onions/scallions, white and green parts separated, shredded

2 tbsp sesame seeds

chilli sauce, to serve

MARINADE
4 tbsp light soy sauce

1 tbsp palm sugar or soft light brown sugar

2 cloves garlic, sliced

5cm/2in piece fresh ginger, finely chopped

1 tbsp sesame oil

Mix together the ingredients for the marinade in a shallow dish. Add the pork and turn until coated. Leave to marinate for at least 1 hour. Drain, reserving the marinade.

Heat a wok until hot. Add the oil, then add half of the pork and stir-fry it for 3–4 minutes until browned. Remove with a slotted spoon and set on one side. Repeat with the remaining pork.

Put the white part of the spring onions/scallions into the wok and stir-fry for 30 seconds, then pour in the reserved marinade and heat through. Return the pork to the wok and stir-fry for 1–2 minutes until the meat is coated in a glossy sauce. Serve sprinkled with the green part of the spring onions/scallions and sesame seeds, with a bowl of chilli sauce on the side.

CRISPY PORK BALLS WITH SPINACH

PREPARATION TIME: 20 minutes, plus 30 minutes chilling

COOKING TIME: 20 minutes   SERVES 4

500g/1lb 2oz lean pork loin fillets, roughly chopped

2 bird's eye chillies, deseeded and thinly sliced

5cm/2in piece fresh ginger, peeled and chopped

handful of fresh coriander/cilantro leaves, roughly chopped

2 sticks lemongrass, peeled and finely chopped

4 spring onions/scallions, chopped

4 tbsp groundnut oil

3 cloves garlic, finely chopped

2 tsp mustard seeds

½ tsp chilli powder

500g/1lb 2oz fresh spinach, tough stalks removed

4 tbsp Chinese rice wine or dry sherry

3 tbsp light soy sauce

1 tsp sugar

juice of 2 limes

salt and freshly ground black pepper

Put the pork, bird's eye chillies, ginger, coriander/cilantro leaves, lemongrass and spring onions/scallions in a food processor and process to form a coarse paste. Season to taste with salt and pepper, then form into 16 walnut-sized balls and chill in the refrigerator for 30 minutes.

Heat half of the oil in a wok and fry the pork balls, four at a time, for 4 minutes, turning occasionally, until golden. Add more oil if necessary before cooking the next batch and keep the cooked balls warm while cooking the remainder.

Wipe the wok clean, pour in the remaining oil and heat. Add the garlic and mustard seeds and stir-fry for 30 seconds, then add the chilli powder, spinach, rice wine, soy sauce and sugar. Stir-fry for 2 minutes, then add the lime juice. Season to taste with salt and pepper and serve, topped with the warm pork balls.

MALAYSIAN PORK WITH BAMBOO SHOOTS

PREPARATION TIME: 20 minutes

COOKING TIME: 25 minutes   SERVES 4

4 tbsp groundnut oil

650g/1lb 7oz lean pork loin fillet, sliced into 2cm/¾in strips across the grain

1 large onion, finely sliced

2 sticks lemongrass, peeled and finely chopped

3 cloves garlic, chopped

½ tsp dried chilli/hot pepper flakes

2 carrots, thinly sliced diagonally

175g/6oz canned bamboo shoots, drained and rinsed

400g/14oz can coconut milk

REMPEH PASTE

1 tsp vegetable oil

6 Asian red shallots, chopped

1 tsp ground turmeric

3 candlenuts or blanched almonds

1 tsp ground coriander

4 red bird's eye chillies, chopped

3 fresh green chillies, chopped

2 pandanus leaves or a few drops vanilla extract

salt

To make the rempeh paste, put all the ingredients in a food processor or blender and process to form a coarse paste. Set on one side.

Heat a wok until hot. Add the oil, then add half the pork and stir-fry for 3–4 minutes until browned. Remove from the wok using a slotted spoon, drain on paper towels and set on one side. Repeat with the remaining pork.

Pour off all but 2 tablespoons of the oil, put the onion into the wok and stir-fry for 3 minutes. Add the lemongrass, garlic and chilli/hot pepper flakes and stir-fry for a further 30 seconds. Add half of the rempeh paste, then the carrots and stir-fry for 2 minutes, then toss in the bamboo shoots and cook for another minute. (The rest of the paste can be stored in the refrigerator for another recipe.)

Pour in the coconut milk and return the pork to the wok. Bring to the boil, then reduce the heat and simmer, covered, for 8 minutes, adding a little water if the sauce appears too dry. Season to taste with salt and serve.

JAPANESE BEEF WITH LIME & SESAME MARINADE

PREPARATION TIME: 15 minutes, plus 30 minutes marinating

COOKING TIME: 3 minutes   SERVES 4

650g/1lb 7oz lean beef fillet, thinly sliced
across the grain

1½ tbsp sunflower oil

2 handfuls of beansprouts

2 tbsp sesame seeds

MARINADE

1 tsp sansho pepper or ground black pepper

2 tsp sesame oil

4 tbsp Japanese soy sauce

2 tbsp mirin or dry sherry

juice of 2 limes

Mix together the ingredients for the marinade in a shallow dish. Add the strips of beef and turn to coat them in the marinade. Leave to marinate for 30 minutes.

Heat a wok until hot, then add the sunflower oil. Lift the beef out of the marinade with a slotted spoon, add to the wok and stir-fry for 1–2 minutes until browned. Add the beansprouts and the marinade and stir-fry for another 1 minute. Serve with the sesame seeds sprinkled over.

BRAISED BEEF WITH BUTTERNUT SQUASH

PREPARATION TIME: 15 minutes

COOKING TIME: 2 hours   SERVES 4

3 tbsp sunflower oil

600g/1lb 5oz chuck steak or beef brisket, cut into 2cm/¾in cubes

2 onions, sliced

3 star anise

1 tsp Chinese five-spice

5cm/2in piece fresh ginger, peeled and finely sliced

4 tbsp dark soy sauce

5 tbsp Chinese rice wine or dry sherry

1 butternut squash, about 750g/1lb 10oz, peeled, deseeded and cubed

salt and freshly ground black pepper

Heat a wok until hot. Add 2 tablespoons of the oil, then add half of the beef and sear until browned all over. Remove the beef using a slotted spoon and set on one side. Repeat with the remaining beef.

Add the remaining oil to the wok with the onions and stir-fry over a medium heat for 5 minutes. Add the star anise, five-spice and ginger and stir-fry for a further minute.

Add 400ml/14fl oz/1½ cups water, the soy sauce and wine, then add the beef and squash. Bring to the boil, reduce the heat, cover and simmer for 1½ hours until the meat is tender. Stir occasionally and add extra water if needed. If there is too much liquid, remove the lid and cook until reduced and thickened. Season to taste with pepper and serve.

Pictured on page 76

BEEF RENDANG

PREPARATION TIME: 25 minutes

COOKING TIME: 2 hours, 25 minutes   SERVES 4

2 tbsp groundnut oil

1 large onion, finely chopped

600/1lb 5oz chuck steak or lean beef brisket, cut into 2.5cm/1in cubes

5 cloves garlic, chopped

5cm/2in piece fresh ginger, peeled and finely chopped

2 sticks lemongrass, peeled and bruised

3 small red chillies, deseeded and finely chopped

4 cardamom pods, split

2 tsp ground turmeric

1 tsp ground coriander

1 tsp chilli powder

1 tsp ground cumin

350ml/12fl oz/1½ cups coconut milk

2 tbsp ground almonds

2 tbsp desiccated/dried shredded coconut, toasted

salt

Heat a wok until hot. Add the oil, then toss in the onion and stir-fry for 4 minutes until softened. Add half of the beef and sear on each side for 1–2 minutes until browned all over. Remove from the wok with a slotted spoon and set on one side. Sear the remaining beef, then return the first batch of beef to the wok. Add the garlic, ginger, lemongrass, chillies and spices and cook, stirring, for 1 minute.

Pour in 400ml/14fl oz/1¾ cups water and the coconut milk. Bring to the boil, then reduce the heat to very low, cover, and simmer for 2 hours. Stir occasionally and add extra water if the curry seems too dry.

Uncover, stir in the almonds and cook for 5–10 minutes. Season to taste with salt and serve, sprinkled with the toasted coconut.

HOISIN BEEF STIR-FRY

PREPARATION TIME: 10 minutes

COOKING TIME: 15 minutes   SERVES 4

6 tbsp hoisin sauce

2 tbsp oyster sauce

2–3 tbsp sunflower oil

500g/1lb 2oz minced/ground beef

1 large onion, finely chopped

2 carrots, diced

handful of fine green beans, trimmed and sliced diagonally

2 cloves garlic, chopped

5cm/2in piece fresh ginger, finely chopped

Mix together the hoisin sauce, oyster sauce and 175ml/6fl oz/¾ cup water in a small bowl.

Heat a wok until hot. Add the oil, then add the beef and stir-fry until browned. Remove from the wok using a slotted spoon and set on one side.

Add more oil to the wok if necessary, then toss in the onion and stir-fry for 4 minutes. Add the carrots and beans and stir-fry for 2 minutes, then add the garlic and ginger and stir-fry for 1 minute.

Pour in the hoisin sauce mixture, stir in the beef and cook for 3 minutes. Serve immediately.

SPICED MEATBALLS IN RED CURRY SAUCE

PREPARATION TIME: 25 minutes, plus 30 minutes chilling

COOKING TIME: 26 minutes   SERVES 4

4 shallots, chopped

2 cloves garlic, chopped

5cm/2in piece fresh ginger, peeled and finely chopped

1 tsp ground cumin

juice of 1 lemon

large handful of fresh coriander/cilantro, finely chopped

1 small free-range egg, lightly beaten

400g/14oz lean minced/ground beef

salt and freshly ground black pepper

RED CURRY SAUCE

2 tbsp sunflower oil

1 large onion, chopped

2 tbsp tandoori curry powder

400g/14oz can chopped tomatoes

300ml/10½fl oz/1¼ cups coconut milk

Place the shallots, garlic, ginger, cumin, lemon juice, coriander/cilantro, egg and minced/ground beef in a food processor and process to form a coarse paste. Season well with salt and pepper, then shape the mixture into about 20 walnut-size balls. Place on a plate and leave to chill, covered, in the refrigerator for about 30 minutes.

To make the sauce, heat the oil in a wok, add the onion and stir-fry for 5 minutes. Add the curry powder and cook for 30 seconds, stirring. Stir in the chopped tomatoes, coconut milk and 6 tablespoons of water. Season to taste, if necessary, with salt and pepper and bring to the boil, then reduce the heat.

Add the prepared meatballs to the sauce, cover and simmer for 20 minutes, turning occasionally, until the meatballs are cooked.

TERIYAKI-STYLE BEEF

PREPARATION TIME: 15 minutes, plus 1 hour marinating

COOKING TIME: 8 minutes   SERVES 4

4 tbsp light soy sauce

2 tbsp sake

4 tbsp mirin or dry sherry

2 tsp sugar

600g/1lb 5oz lean beef sirloin, thinly sliced across the grain

2 tbsp sunflower oil

1 tsp sesame oil

2 cloves garlic, chopped

5cm/2in piece fresh ginger, peeled and finely chopped

280g/10oz fresh spinach, tough stalks removed

4 spring onions/scallions, white and green parts separated, sliced diagonally

1 tbsp sesame seeds

Mix together the soy sauce, sake, mirin and sugar in a shallow bowl. Add the beef and stir well until it is coated, then leave to marinate for 1 hour. Remove the beef from the marinade using a slotted spoon and reserve the marinade.

Heat a wok until hot. Add the oils, then add half of the beef and stir-fry for 1–2 minutes until browned. Remove from the wok using a slotted spoon and set on one side. Repeat with the remaining beef. While the second batch of beef is cooking, heat the marinade in a small saucepan until reduced and slightly syrupy, stirring occasionally.

Add the garlic, ginger, spinach and white part of the spring onions/scallions to the hot wok and stir-fry for 1 minute. Return the beef to the wok with the marinade. Toss well until the beef is coated in the glossy sauce and serve immediately, sprinkled with sesame seeds and the green part of the spring onions/scallions.

AROMATIC CHILLI BEAN LAMB

PREPARATION TIME: 15 minutes, plus 1 hour marinating

COOKING TIME: 10 minutes   SERVES 4

1 tbsp black vinegar

6 tbsp Chinese rice wine or dry sherry

2 tsp palm sugar or soft light brown sugar

3 tbsp light soy sauce

650g/1lb 7oz lean lamb loin fillet, thinly sliced across the grain

2 tbsp sunflower oil

300g/12oz Chinese leaves, stalks sliced

3 cloves garlic, chopped

5cm/2in piece fresh ginger, peeled and chopped

2 tbsp chilli bean paste

Mix together the black vinegar, wine, sugar and soy sauce in a shallow dish. Add the lamb and turn until coated. Leave to marinate for at least 1 hour. Drain, reserving the marinade.

Heat a wok until hot. Add the oil, then add half of the lamb and stir-fry for 2 minutes until browned. Remove using a slotted spoon and set on one side. Repeat with the remaining lamb.

Add the Chinese leaves, garlic and ginger to the wok and stir-fry for 2 minutes. Pour in the reserved marinade and 6 tablespoons of water, then add the bean paste and cook for 2 minutes, stirring frequently, until the liquid has reduced and thickened.

SPICY LAMB STIR-FRY WITH COCONUT RELISH

PREPARATION TIME: 20 minutes, plus 1 hour chilling

COOKING TIME: 12 minutes   SERVES 4

2 tbsp sunflower oil

600g/1lb 5oz lean lamb fillet, thinly sliced across the grain

1 large onion, sliced

1 red pepper, deseeded and sliced

3 cloves garlic, chopped

1 tbsp cumin seeds

1 tbsp mustard seeds

salt and freshly ground black pepper

COCONUT RELISH

40g/1½oz/½ cup desiccated/dried shredded coconut

2 green chillies, finely chopped

2 handfuls of fresh coriander/cilantro, roughly chopped

150ml/5fl oz/⅔ cup natural yogurt

juice of 1 lemon

½ tsp salt

Put the relish ingredients in a food processor and process until combined. Transfer to a bowl and leave in the fridge for 1 hour to allow the relish to thicken.

Heat a wok until hot. Add the oil, then add half of the lamb and stir-fry for 2 minutes. Remove from the wok using a slotted spoon and set on one side. Repeat with the remaining lamb.

Put the onion into the wok and stir-fry for 3 minutes. Add the pepper, garlic and cumin and mustard seeds and stir-fry for a further 2 minutes. Return the lamb to the wok and stir-fry for 2 minutes, adding a little water if the stir-fry is too dry. Season to taste with salt and pepper and serve with the chilled coconut relish.

LAMB ROGAN JOSH

PREPARATION TIME: 20 minutes

COOKING TIME: 1 hour 20 minutes   SERVES 4

700g/1lb 9oz boneless leg of lamb, fat trimmed and cut into 2cm/¾in cubes

1 tsp chilli powder

1 tsp salt

2 tbsp groundnut oil

2 onions, finely chopped

4 cardamom pods, split

2 bay leaves

125ml/4fl oz/½ cup natural yogurt

4 large tomatoes, deseeded and finely chopped

2 tsp tamarind paste

ROGAN JOSH PASTE

2 tsp coriander seeds, crushed

1 tsp mustard seeds, crushed

2 tsp cumin seeds, crushed

2 long red chillies, deseeded and chopped

5cm/2in piece fresh ginger, peeled and chopped

3 cloves garlic, chopped

2 cloves, crushed

1 tsp black peppercorns, crushed

1 small cinnamon stick, crushed

2 tsp paprika

1 tsp salt

1 tsp groundnut oil

To make the rogan josh paste, put the coriander, mustard and cumin seeds in a dry wok and heat gently for 1 minute until they smell aromatic. Allow to cool a little, then put with the rest of the ingredients in a food processor or blender. Add 6 tablespoons of water and process to form a coarse paste. Set on one side.

Put the lamb in a bowl with the chilli powder and salt and turn the meat until well coated.

Heat a wok until hot. Add the oil, then toss in the onions and stir-fry for 5 minutes. Add the cardamom pods, bay leaves and lamb and stir-fry over a medium-high heat for 2 minutes until the meat is browned all over.

Reduce the heat, stir in the rogan josh paste and cook for 3 minutes. Add the yogurt, tomatoes, tamarind paste and 1 litre/35fl oz/4⅓ cups of hot water. Bring to the boil, lower the heat, cover and simmer for 1 hour or until the meat is tender.

Remove the lid and cook for a few minutes until the sauce has reduced and thickened. Serve.

POLTRY

Poultry, particularly chicken, is perfect for stir-frying in a wok, as it is quick to cook, is low in fat and its mild taste readily takes on the flavours of any aromatics that are cooked with it. The fragrant scent of herbs, such as basil and coriander/cilantro, as well as the tang of lemongrass and garlic and the warming intensity of ginger and other pungent spices, all work well with chicken.

In this chapter, alongside classics such as Red-cooked Chicken and Chilli Chicken & Black Bean Stir-fry, you will find interesting twists on traditional combinations, such as Sticky Duck & Orange Stir-fry and Turkey & Mango Stir-fry.

Lighter dishes are represented by Poached Chicken & Vegetables, in which the meat is cooked in a fragrant broth with asparagus, mangetout/snow peas and carrots, and by the simple Steamed Ginger Chicken, infused with the sweetness of fresh basil. Curry-lovers will find plenty to tempt them with a Duck Green Curry or the Lao Chicken & Green Beans, and there's also a recipe for smoking poussin in your wok, which imparts a rich deep smoky flavour.

SHREDDED CHICKEN WITH CORIANDER

PREPARATION TIME: 10 minutes, plus 1 hour marinating

COOKING TIME: 10 minutes   SERVES 4

700g/1lb 9oz skinless chicken breasts, sliced
into strips

2 tbsp groundnut oil

175g/6oz fine green beans, trimmed and halved

large handful of coriander/cilantro leaves

MARINADE

2 tbsp groundnut oil

2 tsp cumin seeds, toasted

2 cloves garlic, crushed

juice and zest of 2 limes

salt and freshly ground black pepper

Mix together the ingredients for the marinade and season well with salt and pepper. Add the chicken and spoon over the marinade. Marinate for at least 1 hour. Drain, reserving the marinade.

Heat a wok until hot. Add the oil, then toss in half of the chicken and stir-fry for 3–4 minutes until lightly browned. Remove the chicken using a slotted spoon, drain on paper towels and keep warm. Repeat with the remaining chicken.

Put the green beans into the wok and stir-fry for 2–3 minutes. Pour in the reserved marinade, then return the chicken to the wok and heat through over a medium heat. Add a little water if the mixture becomes too dry. Serve, sprinkled with the coriander/cilantro leaves.

POACHED CHICKEN & VEGETABLES

PREPARATION TIME: 15 minutes

COOKING TIME: 27 minutes   SERVES 4

4 skinless chicken breasts, about 175g/6oz each

6 tbsp Chinese rice wine or dry sherry

6 tbsp chicken stock

1 large onion, quartered

3 cloves garlic, sliced

5cm/2in piece fresh ginger, peeled and sliced

2 handfuls of mangetout/snow peas, trimmed

12 stalks asparagus, trimmed

2 carrots, sliced into ribbons using a vegetable peeler

light soy sauce, to taste

3 spring onions/scallions, shredded

1 fresh red chilli, deseeded and shredded

Put the chicken in a large wok with the wine, stock, onion, garlic and ginger. Bring to the boil, then reduce the heat and simmer, covered, for 15–20 minutes until the chicken is cooked and there is no trace of pink in the centre. Remove the chicken from the wok with a slotted spoon, set on one side and keep warm.

Add the vegetables to the poaching liquid in the wok and simmer for 4–5 minutes until they are tender. Scoop out the vegetables with a slotted spoon and divide between four warm, shallow serving bowls.

Slice the chicken breasts and place on top of the vegetables, then spoon over any remaining poaching liquid. Drizzle with soy sauce to taste, then garnish with the spring onions/scallions and chilli and serve.

CHILLI CHICKEN & BLACK BEAN STIR-FRY

PREPARATION TIME: 15 minutes, plus 10 minutes soaking

COOKING TIME: 10 minutes   SERVES 4

4 tbsp fermented dried black beans

1 tbsp cornflour/cornstarch

1 tbsp light soy sauce

125ml/4fl oz/½ cup hot chicken stock

2 tbsp sunflower oil

700g/1lb 9oz skinless, boneless chicken thighs, cut into large, bite-size pieces

1 onion, sliced

3 spring onions/scallions, sliced

2 cloves garlic, chopped

5cm/2in piece fresh ginger, peeled and cut into thin strips

2 medium red chillies, deseeded and finely chopped

1 green pepper, deseeded and cut into bite-size pieces

½ tsp Chinese five-spice

1 tsp sesame oil

salt and freshly ground black pepper

Put the black beans into a bowl, cover with hot water and leave to soak for 10 minutes until softened. Drain and set on one side. Mix the cornflour/cornstarch and soy sauce into the hot stock and set on one side.

Heat a wok until hot. Add the oil, then toss in the chicken and stir-fry for 4 minutes until browned. Add the onion and stir-fry for 3 minutes, then add the spring onions/scallions, garlic, ginger, chillies and green pepper and stir-fry for 1 minute, taking care that the garlic does not burn.

Add the soaked black beans, the five-spice and the stock and soy sauce mixture. Cook gently, stirring, until the sauce has thickened, then stir in the sesame oil. Season to taste with salt and pepper and serve.

Pictured on page 100

STEAMED GINGER CHICKEN

PREPARATION TIME: 10 minutes, plus 30 minutes marinating

COOKING TIME: 23 minutes   SERVES 4

2 tbsp sesame oil

7cm/3in piece fresh ginger, peeled and grated

½ tsp Chinese five-spice

3 tbsp light soy sauce

4 skinless chicken breasts, about 175g/6oz each

2 tbsp sunflower oil

16 large basil leaves

salt and freshly ground black pepper

Mix together the sesame oil, ginger, five-spice and soy sauce in a shallow dish. Place the chicken breasts in the dish and spoon the marinade over until the chicken is coated. Leave to marinate for at least 30 minutes.

Meanwhile, heat the oil in a wok and fry the basil leaves for a few seconds until beginning to crisp. Remove the leaves from the wok using a slotted spoon, drain on paper towels and set on one side.

Take four pieces of baking parchment, each large enough to wrap around a chicken breast. Place a chicken breast on top of each one. Spoon the marinade over the chicken and season with salt and pepper. Fold up the paper around the chicken to make four loosely wrapped parcels.

Place the parcels in a large bamboo steamer. Cover and steam over a wok of simmering water for 15–20 minutes or until the chicken is cooked.

Remove the chicken parcels from the steamer and place on four warm serving plates. Open each parcel, sprinkle over the basil leaves and serve.

THAI CHICKEN BITES WITH PAK CHOI

PREPARATION TIME: 25 minutes, plus 30 minutes chilling

COOKING TIME: 40 minutes   SERVES 4

500g/1lb 2oz skinless chicken breasts, chopped

3 cloves garlic, chopped

5cm/2in piece fresh ginger, peeled and grated

5 spring onions/scallions, chopped

1 tbsp Thai fish sauce

1 long red chilli, finely chopped

2 tbsp fresh breadcrumbs

handful of fresh coriander/cilantro leaves, roughly chopped

4 pak choi/bok choy, halved lengthways

2 spring onions/scallions, shredded

4 tbsp sweet chilli sauce

salt and freshly ground black pepper

Place the chicken, garlic, ginger, spring onions/scallions, fish sauce, chilli, breadcrumbs and coriander/cilantro in a food processor or blender and process to form a coarse paste. Season well with salt and pepper and form the paste into 20 walnut-size balls. Put the balls on a plate, cover and chill in the refrigerator for 30 minutes.

Place a lightly oiled plate in a large bamboo steamer. Place half of the balls on the plate, cover and steam over a wok of simmering water for about 15–20 minutes until thoroughly cooked. Remove from the steamer and keep warm. Repeat with the remaining balls.

Meanwhile, steam the pak choi/bok choy for 2–3 minutes in a stacked bamboo steamer or separate pan until tender.

Serve the chicken balls, sprinkled with the shredded spring onions/scallions and accompanied by the pak choi/bok choy and a spoonful of sweet chilli sauce per person.

LAO CHICKEN & GREEN BEANS

PREPARATION TIME: 15 minutes

COOKING TIME: 25 minutes   SERVES 4

3 tbsp groundnut oil

650g/1lb 7oz skinless, boneless chicken thighs, cut into bite-size pieces

6 Asian red shallots, chopped

4 garlic cloves, chopped

7cm/3in piece fresh ginger, peeled and grated

2 red chillies, deseeded and chopped

2 handfuls of fine green beans, trimmed and sliced

12 chestnut/cremini mushrooms, halved or quartered if large

1 tbsp Thai fish sauce

400g/14fl oz coconut milk

juice of 1 lime

handful of fresh coriander/cilantro, roughly chopped

salt

Heat a large wok until hot. Add 2 tablespoons of the oil, then add the chicken and stir-fry for 3–4 minutes until lightly browned. Transfer to a plate lined with paper towels and keep warm.

Put the shallots into the wok and stir-fry for 2 minutes. Add the garlic, ginger and chillies and stir-fry for a further minute. Remove the shallot mixture from the wok and set on one side.

Add more oil to the wok if necessary, then toss in the beans and mushrooms and stir-fry for 3 minutes. Return the chicken and shallot mixture to the wok and stir in the fish sauce and coconut milk. Bring to the boil then reduce the heat to low and simmer for 12–15 minutes until the chicken is tender.

Stir in the lime juice, season to taste with salt and serve, sprinkled with the coriander/cilantro.

RED-COOKED CHICKEN

PREPARATION TIME: 10 minutes, plus 5 minutes infusing

COOKING TIME: 25–45 minutes   SERVES 4

250ml/9fl oz/1 cup dark soy sauce

6 tbsp Chinese rice wine or dry sherry

4 star anise

2.5cm/1in piece fresh ginger, peeled and thinly sliced

4 whole cloves

2 cinnamon sticks

grated zest of ½ lemon or orange

juice of 1 lemon or orange

1 tsp sugar

4 skinless chicken breasts, about 175g/6oz each

Put the soy sauce, wine, star anise, ginger, cloves, cinnamon, zest, juice and sugar in a large wok and bring to the boil. Turn off the heat and set aside for 5 minutes to allow the flavours to infuse.

Add the chicken to the wok, spoon over the liquid, making sure the chicken is covered. Bring to the boil, then reduce the heat and simmer, covered, for 15–20 minutes, turning the chicken halfway through the cooking time and occasionally spooning over the sauce. You may need to cook the chicken in batches.

Serve each chicken breast with a little of the sauce spooned over. The remaining sauce can be chilled or frozen for later use. It makes a good base stock for other poultry and meat dishes.

HOT CHILLI CHICKEN

PREPARATION TIME: 15 minutes, plus 1 hour
   marinating
COOKING TIME: 8 minutes   SERVES 4

700g/1lb 9oz skinless, boneless chicken thighs,
   cut into 1cm/½in strips
2 tbsp sunflower oil
salt and freshly ground black pepper

MARINADE
1 red pepper, deseeded and chopped
2 hot red chillies, finely chopped
2 tsp paprika
4 tbsp red wine vinegar
6 tbsp groundnut oil

Put all the marinade ingredients in a blender or
food processor and purée. Tip into a shallow dish
and add the chicken. Turn the chicken to coat with
the marinade and leave for 1 hour.

Heat a large wok until hot, then add the oil.
Remove the chicken from the marinade using a
slotted spoon, add to the wok and stir-fry for
3–4 minutes.

Reduce the heat and add the remaining marinade.
Season to taste with salt and pepper and cook
the chicken for a further 3 minutes until cooked,
then serve.

SUNSHINE CHICKEN STIR-FRY

PREPARATION TIME: 15 minutes, plus
   30 minutes marinating
COOKING TIME: 5 minutes   SERVES 4

4 tbsp Chinese rice wine or dry sherry
5cm/2in piece fresh ginger, peeled and grated
2 cloves garlic, crushed
500g/1lb 2oz skinless chicken breasts, cut
   into strips
2 tbsp sunflower oil
1 red pepper, deseeded and sliced
1 yellow pepper, deseeded and sliced
½ tsp dried chilli/hot pepper flakes
juice of 1 lemon
grated zest of ½ lemon
2 tbsp light soy sauce

Mix together the wine, ginger and garlic in a
shallow dish. Add the chicken and stir well to
coat it in the marinade. Leave to marinate for
30 minutes.

Heat a wok until hot. Add the oil, then toss in the
red and yellow peppers and the chilli/hot pepper
flakes and stir-fry for 1 minute.

Add the chicken and the marinade and stir-fry for
3 minutes. Add the lemon juice and zest and soy
sauce and stir-fry for another minute, then serve.

WOK-SMOKED POUSSIN

PREPARATION TIME: 25 minutes, plus 1 hour marinating

COOKING TIME: 45–60 minutes   SERVES 4

2 tsp Szechuan peppercorns

1 tsp salt

2 tbsp soft light brown sugar

2 tbsp dark soy sauce

1 poussin

sunflower oil, for brushing

SMOKING MIXTURE

2 large handfuls long-grain white rice

1 large handful black tea leaves

2 tbsp soft brown sugar

1 star anise, broken into bits

Toast the Szechuan peppercorns in a dry wok, then grind using a pestle and mortar. Mix the ground peppercorns with the salt, sugar and soy sauce in a small bowl and set on one side.

To spatchcock the poussin, place it breast-side down on a board. Using kitchen scissors, cut down one side of the backbone, then cut down the other side of the backbone to remove it. Open out the bird, turn it over and flatten by pressing along the breastbone with the flat of your hand. Secure it in the flat position by inserting two skewers, crossing each other, diagonally through the bird.

Put the poussin in a shallow dish and spoon over the Szechuan pepper mixture, rubbing it in well. Leave to marinate, covered, for at least 1 hour in the refrigerator. Bring it back to room temperature before smoking.

Line the inside of the wok and lid with foil to protect it. Mix together the smoking mixture ingredients and put in the base of the wok. Lightly oil a rack with the oil and place it over the smoking mixture, making sure it is not touching.

Heat the wok and when the mixture starts to smoke, put the poussin on the rack and cover with the lid, making sure it is a tight fit and sealing any gaps with crumpled pieces of foil – and open a window.

Reduce the heat to low (but high enough to make sure the mixture is still smoking) and smoke the poussin for 45–60 minutes until it is cooked through and there is no trace of pinkness. Leave to rest for 5 minutes, then remove the poussin from the wok, and serve warm or cold with a vegetable dish or side salad.

FILIPINO TURKEY IN PEANUT SAUCE

PREPARATION TIME: 20 minutes

COOKING TIME: 25 minutes   SERVES 4

115g/4oz fresh shelled peanuts

2 tbsp groundnut oil

650g/1lb 7oz turkey breast or thigh meat, cut into large bite-size pieces

5 shallots, finely chopped

3 cloves garlic, chopped

1 long red chilli, deseeded and chopped

1 tsp hot chilli powder

2 tsp paprika

1 tsp ground turmeric

750ml/26fl oz/3¼ cups hot chicken stock

2 tsp tamarind paste

3 kaffir lime leaves

1 tsp palm sugar or soft light brown sugar

salt and freshly ground black pepper

Heat a large wok, add the peanuts and roast for a few minutes, turning, until lightly browned. Remove from the wok, allow to cool slightly, then grind to a fine powder in a food processor or blender and set on one side.

Heat the oil in the hot wok. Add half the turkey and stir-fry for 3–4 minutes until lightly browned. Remove from the wok using a slotted spoon, drain on paper towels and set on one side. Repeat with the remaining turkey.

Add the shallots and stir-fry for 2 minutes, then add the garlic, chilli, chilli powder, paprika and turmeric and stir-fry for another minute. Pour in the stock, then stir in the tamarind, lime leaves and sugar. Bring to the boil, reduce the heat and simmer for 3 minutes.

Stir in the ground peanuts, season to taste with salt and pepper and simmer for another 6 minutes. Stir in the turkey and simmer for a further 3–4 minutes, stirring occasionally, until heated through and tender, then serve.

TURKEY & MANGO STIR-FRY

PREPARATION TIME: 10 minutes

COOKING TIME: 10 minutes   SERVES 4

2 tbsp sunflower oil

500g/1lb 2oz turkey breast meat, cut into strips

2 cloves garlic, chopped

2 bird's eye chillies, deseeded and finely chopped

juice of 2 limes

1½ tbsp Thai fish sauce

4 spring onions/scallions, sliced diagonally

4 pak choi/bok choy, sliced

1 large mango, pitted, peeled and sliced

large handful of fresh coriander/cilantro,
    roughly chopped

salt

Heat a wok until hot. Add the oil, then add half of the turkey and stir-fry for 3–4 minutes until cooked through and lightly browned. Remove from the wok with a slotted spoon, set on one side and keep warm. Repeat with the remaining turkey.

Add the garlic to the wok with the chillies, lime juice, fish sauce, spring onions/scallions and pak choi/bok choy and stir-fry for 2 minutes.

Return the turkey to the wok with the mango and stir to combine. Season to taste with salt and serve sprinkled with the chopped coriander/cilantro.

TURKEY WITH ROASTED CASHEWS

PREPARATION TIME: 10 minutes

COOKING TIME: 10 minutes   SERVES 4

3 tbsp sunflower oil

large handful of unsalted cashew nuts

600g/1lb 5oz skinless boneless turkey thigh
    meat, cut into bite-size pieces

2 cloves garlic, chopped

7cm/3in piece fresh ginger, peeled and finely
    chopped

2 handfuls of mangetout/snow peas, trimmed

4 tbsp rice wine or dry sherry

2 tbsp light soy sauce

Heat 1 tablespoon of the oil in a wok. Add the cashews and stir-fry until golden. Remove using a slotted spoon, drain on paper towels and set aside.

Pour in the rest of the oil and heat until hot. Add half of the turkey and stir-fry for 3–4 minutes until cooked through and lightly browned. Remove from the wok using a slotted spoon, drain on paper towels and set on one side and keep warm. Repeat with the remaining turkey. Add the garlic, ginger and mangetout/snow peas to the wok and stir-fry for 1 minute. Add the cooked turkey, pour in the wine and soy sauce and stir-fry for a further 1–2 minutes. Serve with the cashew nuts sprinkled over the top.

ORIENTAL TURKEY & MUSHROOM PARCELS

PREPARATION TIME: 20 minutes, plus 30 minutes marinating

COOKING TIME: 30 minutes   SERVES 4

1 tbsp sesame oil

2.5cm/1in piece fresh ginger, peeled and grated

3 tbsp light soy sauce

4 skinless turkey breasts, about 175g/6oz each

1½ tbsp sunflower oil

140g/5oz shiitake mushrooms, sliced

3 spring onions/scallions, sliced diagonally

handful of fresh basil leaves

salt and freshly ground black pepper

Mix together the sesame oil, ginger and soy sauce in a shallow dish. Add the turkey breasts and spoon the marinade over. Leave to marinate for at least 30 minutes, then drain, reserving the marinade.

Heat a wok until hot. Add the oil, then toss in the mushrooms and stir-fry for 2 minutes. Add the spring onions/scallions and stir-fry for 30 seconds, then pour in the marinade, stir, and remove from the heat. Season to taste with salt and pepper.

Make a long slit down the length of each turkey breast and open out to make a pocket, then place each breast on a piece of baking parchment large enough to make a parcel. Spoon a quarter of the mushroom mixture into the pocket of each turkey breast, then spoon over any juices left in the wok and season to taste. Fold the paper up loosely to make four parcels.

Place the turkey parcels in a large bamboo steamer. Cover and steam over a wok of simmering water for 20–25 minutes or until the turkey is cooked and there is no trace of pink in the centre. Remove the parcels from the steamer and place on warming serving plates. Open each parcel and serve with the basil sprinkled over the top.

JAPANESE-STYLE DUCK

PREPARATION TIME: 10 minutes, plus 1 hour marinating

COOKING TIME: 10 minutes   SERVES 4

4 tbsp Japanese soy sauce

4 tbsp mirin

4 tbsp sake

2 tsp sugar

2.5cm/1in piece fresh ginger, peeled and cut into very thin strips

700g/1lb 9oz skinless duck breasts, cut into 1cm/½in strips

2 tbsp sunflower oil

2 spring onions/scallions, shredded

Mix together the soy sauce, mirin, sake, sugar and ginger in a shallow dish. Add the duck strips and turn to coat them in the marinade. Leave to marinate for at least 1 hour. Drain, reserving the marinade.

Heat a wok until hot. Add the oil, then add half of the duck and stir-fry for 3 minutes. Remove from the wok with a slotted spoon and set on one side. Add the remaining duck and stir-fry for 3 minutes.

Return the first batch of duck to the wok, add the reserved marinade and stir-fry until the duck is coated in a glossy sauce. Arrange on a serving plate, scatter over the spring onions/scallions and serve.

DUCK GREEN CURRY

PREPARATION TIME: 15 minutes

COOKING TIME: 30 minutes SERVES 4

2 tbsp sunflower oil

2 large duck breasts, about 250g/9oz each,
     skinned and cut into bite-size pieces

1 medium aubergine/eggplant, cut into cubes

½ quantity Thai Green Curry Paste (see page 154)

400g/14oz can coconut milk

150ml/5fl oz/⅔ cup chicken stock

2 tsp Thai fish sauce

12 cherry tomatoes, halved

juice of 1 lime

handful of fresh Thai basil, roughly chopped

salt and freshly ground black pepper

Heat a large wok until hot. Add the oil, then add the duck and stir-fry for 3 minutes until golden. Remove from the pan using a slotted spoon, drain on paper towels and set aside. Put the aubergine/eggplant into the wok and stir-fry for 6 minutes until lightly browned. Remove and set aside.

Put the curry paste in the wok and cook for 1 minute, stirring. Stir in the coconut milk, stock, fish sauce and duck and bring to the boil. Reduce the heat and simmer for 10 minutes. Add the tomatoes and aubergine/eggplant and cook for a further 5–8 minutes until the sauce has thickened. Stir in the lime juice, season and sprinkle with basil.

STIR-FRIED DUCK WITH CHILLI & MUSHROOMS

PREPARATION TIME: 15 minutes, plus 1 hour
     marinating

COOKING TIME: 8 minutes   SERVES 4

4 tbsp light soy sauce

3 tbsp Shaoxing wine or medium sherry

½ tsp freshly ground black pepper

2 long red chillies, finely sliced

5cm/2in piece fresh ginger, peeled and grated

700g/1lb 9oz skinless duck breasts, cut into
     1cm/½in strips across the grain

6 tbsp sunflower oil

12 shiitake mushrooms, sliced

4 spring onions/scallions, sliced diagonally

Mix the soy sauce, wine, black pepper, chillies and ginger in a dish. Add the duck and spoon over the marinade until well coated. Leave to marinate, covered, in the refrigerator for 1 hour. Drain, reserving the marinade.

Heat a large wok until hot. Add the oil, then add the duck and stir-fry it for 3 minutes. Remove from the wok using a slotted spoon, drain on paper towels, set on one side and keep warm. Pour off all but 2 tablespoons of the oil from the wok. Add the vegetables and stir-fry for 2 minutes. Return the duck to the wok with the reserved marinade. Stir-fry over a high heat until the sauce has reduced.

STICKY DUCK & ORANGE STIR-FRY

PREPARATION TIME: 15 minutes

COOKING TIME: 30 minutes   SERVES 4

juice and finely grated zest of 2 oranges

1 tbsp palm sugar or soft light brown sugar

2.5cm/1in piece fresh ginger, peeled and finely chopped

1 long red chilli, deseeded and cut into rounds

2 star anise

1 tbsp sweet chilli sauce

4 tbsp rice vinegar

4 duck breasts, about 175g/6oz each, skin pricked

handful of fresh coriander/cilantro leaves

3 spring onions/scallions, shredded

Mix together the orange juice and zest, sugar, ginger, chilli, star anise, sweet chilli sauce, rice vinegar and 3 tablespoons of water. Pour the mixture into a large wok, bring to the boil, then reduce the heat and simmer until thickened and syrupy. Pour into a jug and set on one side. Wipe the wok clean.

Add the duck breasts to the wok, skin side down, and sear for 6 minutes on each side. Remove from the wok, leave to rest for 5 minutes in a warm place, then slice.

Pour off all but 1 tablespoon of oil from the wok, add the orange sauce and heat gently until hot. Spoon over the sliced duck, sprinkle with the coriander/cilantro and spring onions/scallions and serve immediately.

FISH & SHELLFISH

All kinds of fish and shellfish can be cooked successfully in a wok. Thick fillets of fish with a firm texture are particularly suited to stir-frying, while whole fish or fillets can be steamed on a rack placed over a wok of simmering water, taking mere minutes. To keep the fish really moist and help retain nutrients, it is often best steamed wrapped in a 'parcel' with a selection of aromatic herbs, slivers of ginger or garlic, or dried spices and a splash of Chinese wine, mirin or soy sauce, to add extra interest and flavour.

A wok can also be used to smoke fish (or meat), giving it a deliciously subtle tang. Any firm fillet of fish can be substituted in the Tea-Smoked Salmon recipe on page 137. In fact, most of the recipes in this chapter can be made using a different type of fish or shellfish from that stated. There are just two things to remember: first, buy the freshest fish or shellfish you can find; second, timing is of the essence – fish and shellfish take only minutes to cook.

The dishes selected for this chapter reflect the popularity of fish and shellfish right across Asia. They range from the creamy coconut curries of southern India to the lemongrass-infused, steamed preparations of Vietnam and the vibrant prawn/ shrimp and scallop stir-fries of China.

GOLDEN FISH WITH SOY & GINGER

PREPARATION TIME: 15 minutes, plus 30 minutes marinating

COOKING TIME: 15 minutes   SERVES 4

2 tbsp cornflour/cornstarch

½ tsp salt

4 tbsp Chinese cooking wine or dry sherry

450g/1lb thick white fish fillets, such as cod, halibut, monkfish or haddock, cut into 2.5cm/1in pieces

3 tbsp plain/all-purpose flour

1 free-range egg white

120ml/4fl oz/½ cup vegetable oil

2 tbsp light soy sauce

1 tsp sugar

2.5cm/1in piece fresh ginger, peeled and finely grated

2 spring onions/scallions, cut into strips

Mix together 1 tablespoon of the cornflour/cornstarch, the salt and the wine in a shallow dish. Add the fish and turn to coat it in the mixture, then leave to marinate for 30 minutes.

Mix together the remaining cornflour/cornstarch and flour on a plate. Beat the egg white in a bowl. Dip the fish pieces into the egg white, then the flour mixture. Heat the oil in a wok until a cube of day-old bread turns golden in 30 seconds. Fry the fish in 2–3 batches until golden, then drain on paper towels and keep warm.

Pour off all but 2 tablespoons of the oil from the wok, then add the soy sauce, sugar, ginger and 150ml/5fl oz/⅔ cup water. Cook until the liquid has reduced slightly. Return the fish to the wok and heat for several minutes until the sauce has almost evaporated. Serve garnished with the spring onion/scallion strips.

INDONESIAN FISH BALLS WITH NUOC CHAM

PREPARATION TIME: 20 minutes, plus 30 minutes chilling
COOKING TIME: 20 minutes   SERVES 4

300g/10½oz pollock or similar white fish fillets,
such as cod or haddock, skinned
300g/10½oz raw prawns/shrimp, peeled
1 large onion, quartered
2.5cm/1in piece fresh ginger, peeled and grated
3 cloves garlic, finely chopped
2 tsp Thai fish sauce
1 tsp sambal oelek (Indonesian chilli sauce) or
1 long red chilli, deseeded and finely chopped
3 tsp kecap manis (Indonesian sweet soy sauce)
finely grated zest of 1 lime
handful of fresh coriander/cilantro, chopped
½ tsp ground turmeric
2 handfuls of fresh breadcrumbs
large pinch of ground cinnamon
1 small free-range egg, lightly beaten
vegetable oil, for deep-frying
handful of fresh basil leaves
salt and freshly ground black pepper

NUOC CHAM
1 clove garlic, chopped
1 small red chilli, deseeded and chopped
2 tsp sugar
juice of 1 lime
2 tbsp rice wine or rice vinegar
2 tbsp Thai fish sauce

Put all the ingredients for the nuoc cham in a blender or food processor with 3 tablespoons of water and process until well combined. Set aside.

Put the fish, prawns/shrimp and onion in a food processor and process to form a coarse paste. Transfer to a bowl and mix in the ginger, garlic, fish sauce, sambal oelek, kecap manis, lime zest, coriander/cilantro, turmeric, breadcrumbs, cinnamon and salt and pepper to taste. Mix in the egg, cover and leave to chill for 30 minutes.

Shape the fish mixture into 20 walnut-size balls. Heat enough oil in a wok to deep-fry the balls, until it is hot enough to brown a day-old cube of bread in about 35 seconds. Add the basil leaves and fry for a few seconds until crisp, then remove and leave to drain on paper towels.

Divide the fish balls into 3 or 4 batches. Add the first batch to the hot oil and fry for 3–4 minutes until golden and cooked through. Remove, drain on paper towels and keep warm. Repeat with the remaining batches of fish balls.

Serve the fish balls, garnished with the basil leaves, and with the nuoc cham.

COCONUT FISH CURRY

PREPARATION TIME: 20 minutes

COOKING TIME: 30 minutes   SERVES 4

1½ tbsp vegetable oil

1 large onion, grated

2 tsp cumin seeds

2 green chillies, finely chopped

2 large cloves garlic, grated

2.5cm/1in piece fresh ginger, peeled and grated

2 tsp ground turmeric

2 tsp ground coriander

2 tsp garam masala

400g/14oz can coconut milk

300g/10½oz canned chopped tomatoes

600g/1lb 5oz skinless haddock or cod fillets, cut into 2.5cm/1in pieces

juice of ½ lemon

handful of fresh coriander/cilantro, roughly chopped

salt and freshly ground black pepper

Heat the oil in the wok. Add the onion and stir-fry for about 4 minutes until it begins to brown. Add the cumin seeds, chillies, garlic, ginger, turmeric, ground coriander and garam masala, then stir-fry for 30 seconds.

Pour in the coconut milk and chopped tomatoes and bring to the boil. Reduce the heat and simmer over a low heat for 15 minutes.

Add the fish and cook for a further 5 minutes, stirring occasionally and taking care not to break up the fish, until the sauce has thickened and the fish is cooked.

Stir in the lemon juice and season to taste with salt and pepper. Spoon into bowls, sprinkle with the chopped coriander/cilantro and serve.

Pictured on page 124

SPICE-BATTERED FISH STICKS WITH SWEET CHILLI MAYO

PREPARATION TIME: 20 minutes

COOKING TIME: 15 minutes   SERVES 4

4 plaice fillets, about 175g/6oz each

115g/4oz/scant 1 cup plain/all-purpose flour

½ tsp paprika

large pinch of salt

1 tbsp vegetable oil, plus extra for deep-frying

2 free-range egg whites

SWEET CHILLI MAYO

4 tbsp mayonnaise

2 tbsp sweet chilli sauce

1 tsp grated fresh ginger

1 mild red chilli, finely chopped

Mix together all the ingredients for the sweet chilli mayo in a small bowl and set on one side. Rinse and pat dry the plaice fillets. Cut each fillet into about 8 strips.

Sift the flour, paprika and salt into a mixing bowl. Gradually beat in the oil and 150ml/5fl oz/ ⅔ cup water. Whisk the egg whites until they form stiff peaks, then fold them into the flour mixture, to form a coating batter.

Pour enough oil into a wok until it is one-third full, then heat the oil until it is hot enough to brown a cube of day-old bread in about 30 seconds. Divide the fish into 4 batches. Cook the first batch by dipping each piece of fish into the batter, then frying in the hot oil for 2–3 minutes until crisp and golden. Drain on paper towels and keep warm. Repeat with the remaining batches of fish. Serve the fish sticks immediately with the sweet chilli mayo dip.

LIME & CHILLI SWORDFISH WITH HERB OIL

PREPARATION TIME: 20 minutes, plus 30 minutes marinating

COOKING TIME: 10 minutes   SERVES 4

4 swordfish steaks, about 175g/6oz each

large handful of fresh mint, roughly chopped

large handful of fresh Thai basil, roughly chopped

large handful of fresh coriander/cilantro, roughly chopped

3 tbsp olive oil

salt and freshly ground black pepper

MARINADE

1 tbsp olive oil

juice and finely grated zest of 2 limes

1 long red chilli, deseeded and thinly sliced

2.5cm/1in piece fresh ginger, peeled and grated

Mix together the ingredients for the marinade in a shallow dish and add the swordfish steaks, turning until well coated. Leave to marinate for 30 minutes.

Make the herb oil by putting the fresh mint, basil and coriander/cilantro with the olive oil in a blender and process until puréed. Season to taste with salt and pepper.

Take the swordfish out of the marinade and put each steak onto a piece of baking parchment large enough to make a parcel. Spoon the marinade over the fish. Fold up the paper around each piece of fish to make a loose parcel.

Place the fish parcels in a large bamboo steamer. Cover and steam over a wok of simmering water for 8–10 minutes or until the fish is cooked.

Remove the fish from the parcels and transfer to warm serving plates. Pour over any juices in the baking paper, then spoon over the prepared herb oil and serve.

VIETNAMESE STEAMED FISH

PREPARATION TIME: 15 minutes

COOKING TIME: 10 minutes   SERVES 4

4 large handfuls of baby spinach leaves, washed

4 thick white fish fillets, such as cod or haddock, about 175g/6oz each

2 sticks lemongrass, peeled and chopped

2 handfuls of fresh mint, chopped

2.5cm/1in piece fresh ginger, peeled and cut into thin strips

2 handfuls of fresh basil, chopped, plus extra to garnish

4 tsp olive oil

4 tsp light soy sauce

salt and freshly ground black pepper

Cut out four pieces of baking parchment, each large enough to wrap around one of the fish fillets and make a parcel. Divide the spinach leaves equally between the four pieces of baking parchment, then place a piece of fish on top.

Mix together the lemongrass, mint, ginger and chopped basil, and sprinkle equal amounts over each fish fillet. Spoon over the oil and soy sauce and season to taste with salt and pepper. Fold up the baking parchment around each piece of fish and its accompaniments to make a loose parcel.

Place the fish parcels in a single layer in a large bamboo steamer. Cover and steam over a wok of simmering water for about 8–10 minutes or until the fish is cooked.

Remove the fish parcels from the steamer and place on four warm plates. Open each parcel and serve with extra fresh basil sprinkled over.

SPICED MARINATED TUNA

PREPARATION TIME: 10 minutes, plus 30 minutes marinating

COOKING TIME: 5 minutes   SERVES 4

3 tbsp sunflower oil

1 tsp ground coriander

1 tsp ground cumin

juice of 1 lemon

4 tuna steaks, about 150g/5½oz each

handful of fresh coriander/cilantro leaves

salt and freshly ground black pepper

Mix together 1 tablespoon of the oil, the ground spices and the lemon juice in a shallow dish. Season to taste with salt and pepper and add the tuna, turning until well coated. Leave to marinate for 30 minutes.

Heat the remaining oil in a wok. Take the tuna out of the marinade using a fish slice and place in the wok. Sear for about 1 minute each side, depending on the thickness of the fish, so that it is still pink in the centre.

Pour in the marinade and heat through. Serve garnished with coriander/cilantro leaves.

TEA-SMOKED SALMON

PREPARATION TIME: 15 minutes, plus 1 hour marinating

COOKING TIME: 35 minutes   SERVES 4

2 tsp Szechuan peppercorns, toasted and crushed

½ tsp Chinese five-spice

1 tsp salt

3 tsp soft brown sugar

4 salmon fillets, about 150g/5½oz each

sunflower oil, for greasing

SMOKING MIXTURE

2 large handfuls of long-grain white rice

large handful of black tea leaves

2 tbsp soft brown sugar

Mix the Szechuan pepper, five-spice, salt and sugar together. Put the salmon fillets in a shallow dish and spoon over the spice and sugar mixture, pressing it into the fish. Leave to marinate for at least 1 hour or preferably overnight.

Line the inside of the wok and lid with foil to protect it. Mix the smoking mixture ingredients together and put in the wok. Lightly oil a rack and place it over the smoking mixture, making sure it is not touching.

Heat the wok and when the mixture starts to smoke, put the salmon on the rack and cover with a tightly fitting lid. Seal any gaps around the lid with crumpled pieces of foil.

Reduce the heat to as low as possible, making sure that the mixture in the wok is still smoking, and smoke the fish for 30 minutes. Keep the kitchen well ventilated. Turn off the heat and leave to stand for 5 minutes. Remove the fish from the wok and serve.

GARLIC & LEMON SQUID

PREPARATION TIME: 20 minutes

COOKING TIME: 5 minutes   SERVES 4

750g/1lb 10oz medium squid, gutted and
    cleaned
4 tbsp sunflower oil
4 cloves garlic, chopped
juice of 2 lemons and finely grated zest of 1
2 red bird's eye chillies, deseeded and finely
    sliced
2 handfuls of fresh coriander/cilantro, roughly
    chopped
salt and freshly ground black pepper

Slice each squid into three and separate the
tentacles. Rinse and pat dry on paper towels.

Heat a wok until hot. Add the oil, then add half of
the squid and stir-fry for 1½ minutes. Remove with
a slotted spoon, drain on paper towels and set on
one side. Repeat with the remaining squid. Add
the garlic, lemon zest and chillies and stir-fry for
another 30 seconds. Return the squid to the wok.

Pour in the lemon juice and 3 tablespoons of
water. Season to taste with salt and pepper
and stir-fry for a few seconds to heat through.
Serve immediately, sprinkled with the chopped
coriander/cilantro.

SZECHUAN SQUID

PREPARATION TIME: 25 minutes

COOKING TIME: 6 minutes   SERVES 4

1 tsp Szechuan peppercorns
½ tsp black peppercorns
½ tsp sea salt flakes
2 tbsp sunflower oil
750g/1lb 10oz small squid, gutted and cleaned
2 large handfuls of mangetout/snow peas, sliced
    diagonally in half
1 long red chilli, deseeded and thinly sliced
3 spring onions/scallions, thinly sliced diagonally
4 large handfuls of Chinese leaves, shredded and
    steamed, to serve

Heat a wok over a medium heat and toast the
peppercorns for a few seconds, shaking the pan
continuously, until they start to darken. Put them
into a mortar and coarsely crush with the salt,
using a pestle.

Heat a wok until hot. Add the oil, then add half of
the squid and stir-fry for 1½ minutes. Remove from
the pan with a slotted spoon and keep warm.
Repeat with the remaining squid. Return all of the
squid to the wok and add the crushed pepper
and salt mix, the mangetout/snow peas, chilli
and spring onions/scallions and stir-fry for another
minute. Serve on a bed of the steamed, shredded
Chinese leaves.

STIR-FRIED SCALLOPS IN OYSTER SAUCE

PREPARATION TIME: 10 minutes

COOKING TIME: 5 minutes   SERVES 4

2 tbsp sunflower oil

16 large scallops, rinsed and patted dry

2 courgettes/zucchini, sliced

1 clove garlic, chopped

2 tbsp soy sauce

3 tbsp oyster sauce

handful of fresh coriander/cilantro, roughly
    chopped

Heat the oil in a large wok over a high heat. Add half of the scallops and sear for 1 minute on each side until golden. Remove from the wok with a spatula and keep warm. Repeat with the remaining scallops.

Add the courgettes/zucchini and garlic to the wok and stir-fry for 1 minute. Pour the soy sauce, oyster sauce and 150ml/5fl oz/⅔ cup water into the wok, then cook until the liquid has reduced and thickened.

Arrange the scallops on warmed serving plates, spoon over the courgettes/zucchini and sauce, garnish with the chopped coriander/cilantro and serve.

STIR-FRIED KING PRAWNS WITH MUSTARD SEEDS

PREPARATION TIME: 15 minutes

COOKING TIME: 4 minutes   SERVES 4

2 tbsp groundnut oil

1 tsp black mustard seeds

2 large cloves garlic, finely chopped

15 curry leaves

400g/14oz raw king prawns/shrimp, peeled

½ tsp chilli powder

3 tbsp lemon juice

1 tsp sugar

Heat the oil in a wok. Add the mustard seeds and fry until they start to pop. Stir in the garlic and curry leaves, then add the prawns/shrimp. Stir-fry for 2 minutes until the prawns/shrimp start to turn pink, then mix in the chilli powder, lemon juice and sugar. Stir well and serve immediately.

PRAWNS & SCALLOPS IN YELLOW BEAN SAUCE

PREPARATION TIME: 20 minutes

COOKING TIME: 10 minutes   SERVES 4

2 tbsp sunflower oil

1 tsp sesame oil

8 large scallops cut into thirds, patted dry

300g/10½oz raw king prawns/shrimp, peeled

2 sticks celery, sliced

1 red pepper, deseeded and cut into bite-size pieces

1 carrot, diced

2 spring onions/scallions, sliced diagonally

2 cloves garlic, chopped

2.5cm/1in piece fresh ginger, chopped

2 tbsp Chinese cooking wine or dry sherry

1 tbsp light soy sauce

4 tbsp yellow bean sauce

salt and freshly ground black pepper

Heat the oils in a wok over a high heat. Add the scallops and sear for 1 minute on each side, then remove using a spatula and set on one side. Add the prawns/shrimp to the hot oil and stir-fry for 2 minutes until they start to turn pink. Remove and set on one side.

Add the celery, pepper and carrot and stir-fry for 2 minutes, then add the spring onions/scallions, garlic and ginger and stir-fry for another 30 seconds.

Reduce the heat slightly and stir in the wine, soy sauce and yellow bean sauce. Season to taste with salt and pepper and cook briefly until the sauce has reduced and thickened, adding a little water if the mixture becomes too dry.

Return the prawns/shrimp and scallops to the wok and heat through. Serve immediately.

SINGAPORE CRAB

PREPARATION TIME: 30 minutes

COOKING TIME: 6 minutes   SERVES 4

2 cooked prepared crabs
2 tbsp chilli sauce
4 tbsp tomato ketchup
1 tsp palm sugar or light soft brown sugar
2 tbsp light soy sauce
juice of 1 lime
2 tbsp groundnut oil
3 cloves garlic, finely chopped
2.5cm/1in piece fresh ginger, finely chopped
1 red chilli, deseeded and finely chopped

Scrub the crab shells. Detach the claws and crack them and then cut the bodies in two, or four if large.

Mix together the chilli sauce, ketchup, sugar, soy sauce, lime juice and 150ml/5fl oz/⅔ cup water in a jug.

Heat the oil in a wok, add the garlic, ginger and chilli and stir-fry for a few seconds. Pour in the chilli, ketchup, soy and lime juice mixture, then add the crab to the wok.

Reduce the heat slightly, stir, and simmer the crab in the sauce for 3–5 minutes, until the sauce has reduced and thickened. Serve.

LOBSTER WITH FRAGRANT BUTTER

PREPARATION TIME: 15 minutes

COOKING TIME: 6 minutes SERVES 4

4 tbsp butter

1 tbsp olive oil

5 spring onions/scallions, sliced on the diagonal

2 sticks lemongrass, peeled and finely chopped

2 kaffir lime leaves, finely shredded

6 tbsp Chinese cooking wine or dry sherry

1 tbsp light soy sauce

175ml/6fl oz/¾ cup fish or vegetable stock

2 cooked lobsters, halved lengthways and claws cracked

handful of basil leaves

lime wedges, to serve

Heat 1 tablespoon of the butter and the oil in a wok over a medium-low heat. Add the spring onions/scallions, lemongrass and lime leaves and stir-fry for 2 minutes. Pour in the wine and simmer until reduced by about half, then add the soy sauce and stock.

Increase the heat and cook until the liquid has reduced by half. Stir in the remaining butter, one tablespoon at a time.

Arrange the prepared lobster on a serving platter. Spoon over the warm butter sauce and sprinkle with the basil leaves. Serve immediately with the wedges of lime.

CLAMS IN RED CURRY SAUCE

PREPARATION TIME: 20 minutes, plus 15 minutes soaking

COOKING TIME: 20 minutes   SERVES 4

1.5 kg/3lb 5oz fresh clams, soaked in cold water
for 15 minutes

250ml/9fl oz/1 cup coconut milk

½ recipe quantity Thai Red Curry Paste
(see page 32)

2 tsp Thai fish sauce

1 tsp palm sugar or light soft brown sugar

3 kaffir lime leaves

juice of 1 lime

small basil leaves, to garnish

Scrub, clean and rinse the clams well under cold running water to remove any grit. Discard any with broken shells or those that remain open when tapped. Place the clams in a wok, cover with 250ml/9fl oz/1 cup of water and cook over a high heat, tossing the wok regularly, for a few minutes until the clams open. Lift out the clams with a slotted spoon, discarding any that remain closed, and set on one side. Strain the liquid through a fine sieve and reserve.

Pour the coconut milk into the wok and heat gently until almost boiling. Stir in the curry paste and cook, stirring, over a low heat for 3 minutes. Add the reserved clam cooking liquid, fish sauce, sugar and lime leaves and cook over a low heat for 7 minutes, stirring frequently.

Pour in the lime juice, then toss in the clams and gently warm through. Serve immediately, garnished with the basil leaves.

MUSSELS IN SPICED TOMATO BROTH

PREPARATION TIME: 20 minutes

COOKING TIME: 14 minutes   SERVES 4

2kg/4lb 8oz mussels
1 tbsp sunflower oil
1 large onion, finely chopped
3 cloves garlic, crushed
2 tsp cumin seeds
2 tsp coriander seeds
½ tsp dried chilli/hot pepper flakes
350ml/12fl oz/1½ cups dry white wine
125g/4½oz/heaped ½ cup canned chopped tomatoes
1 tbsp lemon juice
handful of fresh coriander/cilantro, roughly chopped
salt and freshly ground black pepper

Scrub, clean and rinse the mussels well under cold running water. Discard any mussels with broken shells or those that remain open when tapped.

Heat the oil in a large wok, then add the onion and stir-fry for 3 minutes. Add the garlic, cumin, coriander and chilli/hot pepper flakes and stir-fry for another minute.

Increase the heat, pour in the wine and boil for 2 minutes until reduced. Reduce the heat, add the tomatoes and simmer until reduced by a third.

Toss in the mussels, cover the pan, and cook over a medium heat for 5 minutes, shaking the pan occasionally, or until the mussels have opened. Discard any mussels that remain closed.

Stir in the lemon juice and season to taste with salt and pepper. Spoon into four large serving bowls and pour over the sauce. Serve immediately, garnished with the chopped coriander/cilantro.

GOAN-STYLE COCONUT MUSSELS

PREPARATION TIME: 20 minutes

COOKING TIME: 10 minutes   SERVES 4

2kg/4lb 8oz mussels

2 tbsp groundnut oil

2 onions, finely chopped

2.5cm/1in piece fresh ginger, peeled and finely chopped

3 cloves garlic, finely chopped

2 long red chillies, deseeded and finely sliced

½ tsp fenugreek seeds

4 cardamom pods, split

½ tsp cumin seeds

1 tsp ground turmeric

250ml/9fl oz/1 cup coconut milk

2 tbsp lime juice

handful of fresh coriander/cilantro, roughly chopped

salt and freshly ground black pepper

Scrub, clean and rinse the mussels well under cold running water. Discard any mussels with broken shells or those that remain open when tapped.

Heat a wok until hot. Add the oil, then toss in the onion and stir-fry for 2 minutes. Add the ginger and garlic and stir-fry for another 2 minutes. Add the chillies, fenugreek, cardamom and cumin seeds and stir-fry for a further minute. Mix in the turmeric.

Pour in the coconut milk and 120ml/4fl oz/ ½ cup of water and bring to the boil. Add the mussels and lime juice, reduce the heat, cover and cook over a medium heat for 5 minutes or until the mussels have opened. Discard any mussels that remain closed. Season to taste with salt and pepper.

Spoon the mussels into four large serving bowls, and pour over the sauce. Serve immediately, garnished with the chopped coriander/cilantro.

VEGETARIAN

Since stir-fried vegetables are cooked in a matter of minutes, they retain much of their vitamin and mineral content, making it possible to prepare meat-free meals in a wok that are as packed with nutrients as they are appealing to the senses. Asian countries also offer up a treasure trove of vegetarian culinary delights, that are not only quick to prepare but are also highly colourful, rich in flavour and varied in texture, with a deliciously light, fresh quality.

When stir-frying vegetables in a wok, it is important to remember a few rules. Always cut them up into uniform-sized pieces, so that they cook evenly. Add denser vegetables, such as carrots and green beans, to the wok first, as they require a longer cooking time than, say, courgettes/zucchini or beansprouts. And do bear in mind the shape of the vegetable. Cutting long vegetables on the diagonal makes them look more appealing than chunks or slices and creates a bigger surface area, speeding up cooking time.

In addition, a wok can also be used in the same way as the Indian *kadahi* (a wok-shaped pan with round handles on either side) to create fabulously fragrant curries, such as the ever-popular vegetable dahls, as well as Thai green and red curries or a creamy Sri Lankan Egg Curry.

HALF-MOON AUBERGINE WITH CHILLI & GARLIC

PREPARATION TIME: 10 minutes, plus 30 minutes standing

COOKING TIME: 15 minutes   SERVES 4

2 medium aubergines/eggplants, sliced into rounds then halved

4 tbsp sunflower oil

4 cloves garlic, chopped

2 red bird's eye chillies, deseeded and finely chopped

juice of 1 lemon

handful of fresh basil leaves, torn

salt and freshly ground black pepper

Put the aubergine/eggplant pieces on a plate and sprinkle generously with salt. Cover and set aside for 30 minutes. Rinse well, then pat dry with paper towels.

Heat a wok until hot. Add the oil, then toss in half of the aubergine/eggplant and stir-fry for 7 minutes until lightly browned and tender. Remove from the wok with a slotted spoon and set on one side. Add the remaining aubergine/eggplant and stir-fry for 7 minutes.

Return the first batch of aubergine/eggplant to the wok, then toss in the garlic and chillies and stir-fry for 30 seconds. Stir in the lemon juice, season to taste with salt and pepper and serve, sprinkled with the torn basil leaves.

Pictured on page 150

CAULIFLOWER & POTATO KADAHI

PREPARATION TIME: 15 minutes

COOKING TIME: 20 minutes   SERVES 4

2 tbsp groundnut oil

4 green chillies, cut down one side and deseeded

1 large onion, thinly sliced

8 large cauliflower florets, cut into small florets and stalks sliced

8 curry leaves

1 tsp black mustard seeds, crushed

1 tsp cumin seeds

3 cloves garlic, finely chopped

5cm/2in piece fresh ginger, peeled and finely chopped

1 tsp chilli powder

2 large potatoes, peeled, cooked and cut into bite-size pieces

250ml/9fl oz/1 cup vegetable stock

juice of 1 lemon

handful of fresh coriander/cilantro, roughly chopped

salt

Heat a wok until hot. Add the oil, then toss in the chillies and fry them for 1 minute. Remove the chillies from the wok and discard.

Put the onion into the wok and stir-fry for 2 minutes. Add the cauliflower and cook for another 2 minutes. Stir in the curry leaves, mustard seeds and cumin seeds and cook for one more minute. Add the garlic, ginger and chilli powder and stir-fry for a further minute.

Add the potatoes, pour in the stock and lemon juice. Stir and cook over a medium heat until the liquid is reduced. Stir in half of the chopped coriander/cilantro, season to taste with salt, cover and cook over a low heat for 5 more minutes. Serve, sprinkled with the remaining chopped coriander/cilantro.

MIXED MUSHROOM GREEN CURRY

PREPARATION TIME: 15 minutes

COOKING TIME: 20 minutes   SERVES 4

2 tbsp sunflower oil

300ml/10½fl oz/1¼ cups coconut milk

300ml/10½fl oz/1¼ cups vegetable stock

2 tsp vegetarian 'fish' sauce

1 tsp palm sugar or soft light brown sugar

100g/3½oz shiitake mushrooms, halved

100g/3½oz chestnut/cremini mushrooms, halved

1 large red pepper, deseeded and sliced

400g/14oz canned straw mushrooms, drained and rinsed

handful of fresh basil leaves, torn

salt and freshly ground black pepper

THAI GREEN CURRY PASTE

6 green chillies, deseeded and chopped

2 sticks lemongrass, peeled and chopped

2 shallots, peeled and chopped

juice of 2 kaffir limes and zest of 1

3 cloves garlic, chopped

1 tsp ground coriander

1 tsp ground cumin

2.5cm/1in piece fresh ginger, peeled and chopped

large handful of fresh coriander/cilantro, chopped

handful of fresh coriander/cilantro roots, chopped

1 tbsp sunflower oil

1 tsp salt

To make the green curry paste, place all the ingredients in a food processor or blender and process to form a coarse paste.

Heat the oil in a large wok. Add half of the curry paste and stir-fry for 1 minute. (The rest of the paste can be stored in the refrigerator for another recipe.) Stir in the coconut milk and stock and bring to the boil. Stir in the fish sauce and sugar, lower the heat and simmer for 10 minutes until reduced.

Add the shiitake and chestnut/cremini mushrooms and red pepper and cook for 5 minutes, then add the straw mushrooms and cook for another 2 minutes until the vegetables are tender. Season to taste with salt and pepper and serve with the basil leaves sprinkled over the top.

THAI RED BUTTERNUT SQUASH CURRY

PREPARATION TIME: 15 minutes

COOKING TIME: 20 minutes   SERVES 4

2 tbsp groundnut oil

3 Asian red shallots, chopped

3 cloves garlic, chopped

5cm/2in piece fresh ginger, peeled and finely chopped

1 medium butternut squash, about 750g/1lb 10oz peeled, deseeded and cubed

2 kaffir lime leaves

½ tsp ground turmeric

½ recipe quantity Thai Red Curry Paste (see page 32)

400g/14oz can coconut milk

250ml/9fl oz/1 cup vegetable stock

juice of 1 lime

handful of fresh coriander/cilantro leaves

handful of beansprouts

1 large onion, chopped and fried until crisp and golden

salt and freshly ground black pepper

Heat a wok until hot. Add the oil, then toss in the shallots and stir-fry for 1 minute. Add the garlic, ginger, squash and lime leaves and stir-fry for 4 minutes.

Stir in the turmeric and curry paste, then pour in the coconut milk and stock and bring to the boil. Reduce the heat and simmer, covered, for 10 minutes.

Stir in the lime juice, season to taste with salt and pepper and cook for about 2 minutes until the liquid has reduced and thickened. Serve, topped with the coriander/cilantro leaves, beansprouts and crispy onion.

WINTER VEGETABLE STIR-FRY WITH CHILLI CASHEWS

PREPARATION TIME: 15 minutes

COOKING TIME: 8 minutes   SERVES 4

2 tbsp sunflower oil

2 handfuls of unsalted cashew nuts

1 tsp chilli bean paste

6 large cauliflower florets, cut into small florets and stalks sliced

6 large broccoli florets, cut into small florets and stalks sliced

2 carrots, sliced diagonally

2 turnips, peeled and thinly sliced

4 large Chinese leaves, shredded

5cm/2in piece fresh ginger, peeled and chopped

2 tbsp Shaoxing wine or whisky

2 tbsp light soy sauce

1 tsp sesame oil

Heat 1 teaspoon of the sunflower oil in a wok, then toss in the cashew nuts and chilli bean paste and stir-fry for 1 minute. Remove the cashews with a slotted spoon and set on one side.

Wipe the wok, then pour in and heat the remaining sunflower oil. Add the cauliflower and broccoli and stir-fry for 2 minutes. Remove from the wok and set on one side. Put the carrots and turnips into the wok and stir-fry for 2 minutes.

Return the broccoli and cauliflower to the wok with the Chinese leaves and ginger. Stir-fry for 1 minute, then pour in the wine, soy sauce, sesame oil and 2 tablespoons of water. Cook for a further minute and serve with the chilli cashews sprinkled over the top.

VEGETABLE TEMPURA WITH DIP

PREPARATION TIME: 20 minutes

COOKING TIME: 20 minutes   SERVES 4

115g/4oz/scant 1 cup plain/all-purpose flour

½ tsp paprika

large pinch of salt

1 tbsp sunflower oil, plus extra for deep-frying

2 free-range egg whites

650g/1lb 7oz selection mixed vegetables such
  as sweet peppers, cooked potatoes, onion,
  broccoli and cauliflower florets, baby corn
  and mushrooms

DIP

6 tbsp rice vinegar

1 tbsp sugar

1 tbsp dark soy sauce

1 red bird's eye chilli, deseeded and
  finely chopped

juice of 1 lime

handful of fresh coriander/cilantro,
  finely chopped

Make the dipping sauce by heating the rice vinegar, sugar and soy sauce in a small saucepan until it begins to turn syrupy. Remove from the heat, pour into a bowl and leave to cool. When cool, stir in the chilli, lime juice and coriander/cilantro and set on one side.

Sift the flour, paprika and salt into a mixing bowl. Gradually beat in the 1 tablespoon of sunflower oil and 150ml/5fl oz/⅔ cup water. Whisk the egg whites until they form stiff peaks, then fold them into the flour mixture. Set on one side.

Prepare the vegetables. Cut the peppers, onions and potatoes into thick slices, broccoli and cauliflower into medium-sized florets and leave the baby corn and mushrooms whole.

Pour enough sunflower oil into a large wok until it is one-third full. Heat the oil until it browns a cube of day-old bread in about 30 seconds. Divide the vegetables into 3 or 4 batches. Take the first batch and dip each piece of vegetable into the prepared batter, then carefully place in the oil and fry for 2–3 minutes until crisp and golden. Remove from the wok with a slotted spoon, drain on paper towels and keep warm while frying the remaining batches of vegetables.

As soon as the last batch of vegetables is cooked, serve the battered vegetables with the bowl of dipping sauce.

VEGETABLES IN YELLOW BEAN SAUCE

PREPARATION TIME: 10 minutes

COOKING TIME: 5 minutes   SERVES 4

2 tbsp groundnut oil

1 large onion, sliced

16 baby corn

3 handfuls of French beans, trimmed and sliced
    diagonally

2 handfuls of mangetout/snow peas, trimmed

2 courgettes/zucchini, sliced

2 green chillies, deseeded and chopped

2 cloves garlic, chopped

2.5cm/1in piece fresh ginger, peeled and
    chopped

handful of sprouted mixed beans

5 tbsp yellow bean sauce

2 tbsp light soy sauce

Heat a wok until hot. Add the oil, then toss in the
onion and stir-fry for 2 minutes. Add the corn,
beans, mangetout/snow peas, courgettes/
zucchini, chillies, garlic and ginger and stir-fry for
another 2 minutes.

Add the sprouted beans, then pour in the yellow
bean sauce, soy sauce and 3 tablespoons of
water, cook for 1 minute and serve.

VIETNAMESE LEMON-GRASS VEGETABLES

PREPARATION TIME: 10 minutes

COOKING TIME: 8 minutes   SERVES 4

1 tbsp vegetarian 'fish' sauce

1 tbsp rice wine or dry sherry

1 tbsp light soy sauce

1 tsp palm sugar or soft light brown sugar

1 tbsp groundnut oil

1 onion, thinly sliced

2 large cloves garlic, chopped

1 red chilli, deseeded and chopped

2 sticks lemongrass, peeled and finely chopped

3 carrots, sliced diagonally

140g/5oz chestnut/cremini mushrooms, sliced

2 courgettes/zucchini, sliced

2 pak choi/bok choy, sliced

salt and freshly ground black pepper

Mix the fish sauce, rice wine, soy sauce, sugar and
2–3 tablespoons of water in a bowl and set aside.

Heat a wok until hot. Add the oil, then toss in the
onion, garlic, chilli and lemongrass and stir-fry
them for 1 minute. Add the carrots and stir-fry for
2 minutes, then add the mushrooms, courgettes/
zucchini and pak choi/bok choy and stir-fry for
another 2 minutes. Pour in the fish sauce mixture,
stir-fry for 2 minutes, then season to taste with salt
and pepper and serve.

THAI ASPARAGUS ROLLS

PREPARATION TIME: 15 minutes

COOKING TIME: 20 minutes   SERVES 4

12 asparagus spears, trimmed

1 tbsp sesame oil

2 tbsp groundnut oil

2 Asian red shallots, finely chopped

3 spring onions/scallions, finely chopped

1 long red chilli, deseeded and finely chopped

6 large free-range eggs, lightly beaten

large handful of fresh coriander/cilantro, finely chopped

salt and freshly ground black pepper

TO SERVE
2 spring onions/scallions, shredded

1 red chilli, deseeded and cut into fine strips

a handful of fresh coriander/cilantro leaves

Mix the asparagus with the sesame oil in a bowl until well coated. Heat a wok until hot. Toss in the asparagus and stir-fry for 2–3 minutes until tender. Remove from the wok, set aside and keep warm.

Add half the groundnut oil to the wok, then the shallots, finely chopped spring onions/scallions and finely chopped chilli and stir-fry for 1 minute. Remove from the wok, set aside and keep warm.

Season the beaten eggs to taste with salt and pepper, then stir in the finely chopped coriander/cilantro. Add a little more oil to the wok or large frying pan, pour in a quarter of the egg mixture and swirl it around to make a large thin omelette. Cook until set, then slide the omelette onto a plate and set on one side and keep warm. Repeat with the remaining egg mixture to make three more omelettes, adding more oil when necessary.

Spoon a quarter of the shallot mixture down the middle of each omelette, then arrange 3 asparagus spears on top. Roll up the omelettes and cut each roll into 1cm/½in lengths. Divide between four serving plates, sprinkle over the shredded spring onions/scallions, chilli strips and coriander/cilantro leaves and serve.

SRI LANKAN EGG CURRY

PREPARATION TIME: 15 minutes

COOKING TIME: 15 minutes   SERVES 4

2 tbsp groundnut oil

1 large onion, chopped

2 tsp cumin seeds

4 cloves garlic, chopped

2.5cm/1in piece fresh ginger, peeled and chopped

10 curry leaves

4 cardamom pods, split

2 green chillies, sliced

2 tsp chilli powder

1 tsp ground turmeric

3 tomatoes, deseeded and chopped

5 large handfuls of spinach leaves, tough stalks removed

300ml/10½fl oz/1¼ cups coconut milk

6 large free-range eggs, hard-boiled, shelled and halved

large handful of fresh coriander/cilantro, roughly chopped

salt and freshly ground black pepper

Heat the oil in a wok. Add the onion and cumin seeds and stir-fry for 3 minutes. Add the garlic, ginger, curry leaves, cardamom pods and green chillies and stir-fry for 1 minute.

Add the chilli powder, turmeric, tomatoes, spinach, coconut milk and 250ml/9fl oz/ 1 cup of water. Season to taste with salt and pepper and bring to the boil.

Stir, then reduce the heat and simmer for 10 minutes until thickened and reduced. Serve, topped with the hard-boiled eggs and sprinkled with the chopped coriander/cilantro.

JAPANESE NORI EGG ROLL

PREPARATION TIME: 15 minutes

COOKING TIME: 20 minutes   SERVES 4

1 tbsp mirin

1 tbsp Japanese soy sauce or tamari

1 tsp brown miso paste

3 tbsp sunflower oil

225g/8oz long-stem broccoli, florets left whole and stems sliced

1 carrot, cut into thin sticks

2.5cm/1in piece fresh ginger, peeled and grated

2 large cloves garlic, crushed

6 spring onions/scallions, sliced on the diagonal

2 courgettes/zucchini, cut into thin sticks

6 large free-range eggs, lightly beaten

1½ tbsp nori flakes

salt and freshly ground black pepper

Mix together the mirin, soy sauce and miso paste in a small bowl and set on one side.

Heat a wok until hot. Add 2 tablespoons of the oil, then toss in the broccoli and carrot and stir-fry for 2 minutes. Add the ginger, garlic, spring onions/scallions and courgettes/zucchini and stir-fry for 1–2 minutes until tender. Stir in the mirin mixture and cook for 1 minute. Remove from the wok, set on one side and keep warm.

Season the beaten eggs to taste with salt and pepper and stir in the nori flakes. Heat a little of the remaining oil in the wok or a large frying pan and add a quarter of the beaten egg mixture. Swirl it around so that it covers the base of the pan and forms a thin omelette. Cook until set, then turn out onto a plate and keep warm. Use the remaining egg mixture to make three more omelettes, adding more oil to the pan when necessary.

Spoon a quarter of the vegetable stir-fry down the middle of each omelette, roll up loosely and serve.

SAG PANEER

PREPARATION TIME: 10 minutes

COOKING TIME: 15 minutes   SERVES 4

1 tbsp groundnut oil
2 tbsp softened butter
280g/10oz block of paneer
2 onions, chopped
2 cloves garlic, chopped
1 tbsp cumin seeds
1 tsp ground turmeric
500g/1lb 2oz spinach leaves, tough stalks
    removed
salt and freshly ground black pepper

Put the oil and butter in a wok and heat until the butter has melted. Add the paneer and cook until golden on one side, then turn over and cook the second side until golden. Remove from the pan and drain on paper towels. Cut into cubes and set on one side.

Add the onions to the wok and stir-fry for 2 minutes. Add the garlic, cumin seeds and turmeric and cook for another minute, stirring constantly.

Toss in the spinach and 4 tablespoons of water and stir-fry for 2 minutes. Season to taste with salt and pepper and place the paneer on top of the spinach. Cook for about 2 minutes until the paneer melts slightly, then stir it in and serve.

MASOOR DAHL

PREPARATION TIME: 10 minutes

COOKING TIME: 25 minutes   SERVES 4

225g/8oz split red lentils, rinsed
2 tbsp groundnut oil
2 large onions, chopped, and 1 fried until crisp
    and golden
3 cloves garlic, finely chopped
2.5cm/1in piece fresh ginger, peeled and finely
    chopped
2 long red chillies, deseeded and chopped
1 tsp cumin seeds
1 tsp ground turmeric
3 tomatoes, deseeded and chopped
salt

Put the lentils in a saucepan, cover with 600ml/21fl oz/2½ cups of water and bring to the boil. Reduce the heat, half cover the pan, and simmer for 20 minutes, scooping any froth off the top with a spoon. When the lentils are tender and the water has been absorbed, beat the lentils with a wooden spoon until soft and mushy. Set aside.

Heat the oil in a wok. Add the uncooked chopped onion and stir-fry for 5 minutes over a medium heat. Add the garlic, ginger, chillies, cumin and turmeric and cook for another minute.Stir in the tomatoes and cooked lentils, season with salt, and heat through for a few minutes. Serve, topped with the crispy onion.

TEMPEH SATAY STIR-FRY

PREPARATION TIME: 15 minutes

COOKING TIME: 10 minutes   SERVES 4

2 tbsp crunchy peanut butter

2 tbsp soy sauce

2 tsp vegetarian 'fish' sauce

125ml/4fl oz/½ cup creamed coconut

2 tsp palm sugar or brown sugar

2 tbsp sunflower oil

300g/10½oz tempeh, thinly sliced

2 large handfuls of mangetout/snow peas

1 large red pepper, deseeded and sliced

2 long red chillies, deseeded and thinly sliced into rounds

2.5cm/1in piece fresh ginger, peeled and finely chopped

2 cloves garlic, finely chopped

2 spring onions/scallions, sliced

handful of fresh coriander/cilantro, roughly chopped

salt

Mix together the peanut butter, soy sauce, fish sauce, creamed coconut, sugar and 6 tablespoons of hot water in a small bowl and set on one side.

Heat the oil in a wok. Add half the tempeh and fry for 2–3 minutes on each side until lightly browned. Remove from the wok with a spatula, drain on paper towels, set on one side and keep warm. Repeat with the remaining tempeh.

Put the mangetout/snow peas, pepper and chillies into the wok and stir-fry for 1 minute. Add the ginger, garlic and spring onions/scallions and stir-fry for another 30 seconds.

Add the peanut butter mixture, season to taste with salt and stir-fry for 1–2 minutes until the sauce has reduced and thickened. Add more water if the sauce appears too dry.

Arrange the tempeh on a warm serving platter, spoon over the hot sauce, sprinkle with the chopped coriander/cilantro and serve.

TAMARIND TOFU WITH PAK CHOI

PREPARATION TIME: 15 minutes

COOKING TIME: 20 minutes   SERVES 4

125ml/4fl oz/½ cup vegetable stock

1 tsp tamarind paste

1 tsp sugar

2 tbsp light soy sauce

3 tbsp sunflower oil

350g/12oz firm tofu, drained, patted dry and sliced into bars

1 large onion, sliced

3 pak choi/bok choy, sliced

1 large red pepper, deseeded and sliced

5cm/2in piece fresh ginger, peeled and finely chopped

2 cloves garlic, chopped

handful of fresh coriander/cilantro, roughly chopped

salt and freshly ground black pepper

Mix together the stock, tamarind paste, sugar and soy sauce in a small bowl and set on one side.

Heat the oil in a wok. Add half the tofu and fry, turning occasionally, for 4–5 minutes until golden. Drain on paper towels and set on one side. Repeat with the remaining tofu.

Pour off all but 1 tablespoon of the oil from the wok, add the onion and stir-fry for 2 minutes, then add the pak choi/bok choy, red pepper, ginger and garlic and stir-fry for another minute.

Pour the tamarind mixture into the wok and cook for 2 minutes until it is reduced and thickened. Season to taste with salt and pepper. Carefully stir in the tofu, heat through and serve, sprinkled with the chopped coriander/cilantro.

TERIYAKI TOFU & WATER SPINACH

PREPARATION TIME: 15 minutes, plus 1 hour marinating

COOKING TIME: 15 minutes   SERVES 4

350g/12oz firm tofu, drained, patted dry
and cut into cubes

2 tbsp sunflower oil

5cm/2in piece fresh ginger, cut into thin strips

5 Chinese leaves, thinly sliced

6 large handfuls of Chinese water spinach
leaves, sliced

1 large yellow pepper, deseeded and sliced

1 long red chilli, deseeded and sliced into rounds

MARINADE
6 tbsp teriyaki sauce

1 tbsp sesame oil

1 tbsp Japanese soy sauce or tamari

2 tsp sugar

1 tbsp sesame oil

Mix together the ingredients for the marinade in a shallow dish. Add the tofu and turn to coat it in the marinade. Leave to marinate for at least 1 hour. Drain, reserving the marinade.

Heat half of the oil in a wok. Add half the tofu and fry for 2–3 minutes without moving, then carefully turn over and fry the other side, until it is lightly browned all over. Remove from the wok using a spatula, drain on paper towels, set on one side and keep warm. Add the remaining oil to the wok and fry the remaining tofu. Remove from the wok, drain on paper towels and set on one side with the first batch. Reserve the marinade.

Toss the ginger, Chinese leaves, spinach, pepper and chilli into the wok and stir-fry for 2 minutes. Pour in the reserved marinade, then return the tofu to the wok. Stir-fry until the marinade has reduced slightly and thickened, then serve.

INDEX

NOURISH

EAT WELL, LIVE WELL

Here at Nourish we're all about wellbeing through food and drink – irresistible dishes with a serious good-for-you factor. If you want to eat and drink delicious things that set you up for the day, suit any special diets, keep you healthy and make the most of the ingredients you have, we've got some great ideas to share with you. Come over to our blog for wholesome recipes and fresh inspiration – nourishbooks.com